WHY
DO CATS' EYES
GLOW
IN THE DARK?

WHY
DO CATS' EYES
GLOW
IN THE DARK
?

(AND OTHER QUESTIONS KIDS ASK
ABOUT ANIMALS)

JOANNE SETTEL
NANCY BAGGETT

ILLUSTRATED BY LINDA TUNNEY

ATHENEUM / 1988 / NEW YORK

Library of Congress Cataloging-in-Publication Data
Settel, Joanne.
Why do cats' eyes glow in the dark?
Summary: Answers fifty questions about a variety
of vertebrates, such as "Do bats really suck blood?"
and "Can toads give you warts?"
1. Animals—Miscellanea—Juvenile literature.
2. Vertebrates—Miscellanea—Juvenile literature.
[1. Animals—Miscellanea. 2. Vertebrates—Miscellanea.
3. Questions and answers] I. Baggett, Nancy,
1943–   II. Tunney, Linda, ill.   III. Title.
QL49.S416   1988   596   87-13708
ISBN 0-689-31267-9

Atheneum
Macmillan Publishing Company
866 Third Avenue, New York, NY 10022
Collier Macmillan Canada, Inc.

Dedicated to Barry and Roc
for their endless support
and understanding.

CONTENTS

CLASSIFICATION CHART
VERTEBRATES—SUBPHYLUM VERTEBRATA
(Animals with Backbones)

Note: This chart only includes classification of animals that are mentioned in this book.

Superclass: Pisces (fish)
  Class: Osteichthyes (fishes with skeletons made of bone)
  Order: Gasterosteiformes (seahorses)

Superclass: Tetrapoda (four-legged land vertebrates)
  Class: Amphibia (frogs, toads, salamanders, etc.)
  Order: Anura (frogs, toads)

  Class: Reptilia (turtles, crocodiles, snakes, lizards, etc.)
  Order: Lepidosauria (chameleons, rattlesnakes)
  Order: Crocodylia (crocodiles)

Class: Aves (birds)
Order: Galliformes (chickens)
Order: Pelecaniformes (pelicans)
Order: Anseriformes (geese, ducks)
Order: Falconiformes (vultures)
Order: Strigiformes (owls)
Order: Piciformes (woodpeckers)
Order: Psittaciformes (parrots)
Order: Sphenisciformes (penguins)

Class: Mammalia (mammals)
Subclass: Prototheria (egg-laying mammals)
Order: Monotremata (platypus)
Subclass: Theria (non-egg-laying mammals)
Order: Marsupialia (kangaroos, opossums)
Order: Chiroptera (bats)
Order: Carnivora (cats, dogs, skunks, cheetahs)
Order: Rodentia (squirrels, beavers)
Order: Primata (gorillas)
Order: Perissodactyla (zebras)
Order: Artiodactyla (cows, deer, sheep, giraffes,
camels)
Order: Proboscidea (elephants)
Order: Cetacea (whales)

WHY
DO CATS' EYES
GLOW
IN THE DARK?

WHY DO CATS' EYES GLOW IN THE DARK?

A cat's eyes aren't equipped with mirrors, but they do have special mirrorlike cells that cause them to glow in the dark. Cats and other animals that see well in the dark have a structure in the back of each eye called the *tapetum lucidum*. This patch of cells glows whenever it's hit by light.

The tapetum's cells shine because they are filled with a substance called *guanine*. Guanine causes light rays to bounce off its surface, or be *reflected*. When light hits the guanine-filled cells,

the reflected rays flood the eyeball with light. Even the small amounts of light that are present at nighttime are enough to light up a cat's eyes. This makes it possible for cats to see when it seems totally dark to a human.

Humans and other animals with good day vision do not have any reflective tissue in their eyes. Instead, the back of the human eye is covered with a thin layer of black tissue called the *choroid* (kor/ oyd). The choroid absorbs, or soaks up, light rays. It lies just underneath another thin layer of cells called the *retina.* The retina contains the rod and cone cells, which are the light-detecting cells of the eye. When light rays enter the lens at the front of the eye, they are bent so that they all come together, or are *focused.* These focused rays hit the rods and cones and excite them. Then the focused rays hit the black choroid and get absorbed. This keeps light rays from bouncing back again into the eyeball.

If light rays were to bounce back, they would excite the rods and cones again, providing the eye with extra light. However, these reflected rays would not have been bent together by the lens and thus would not be sharply focused. As a result, the eye would see a fuzzy picture. The black choroid makes it possible for human eyes to see objects clearly.

In cats, the black choroid is partially replaced by the tapetum lucidum. Since the tapetum makes light rays bounce around the cat's eyes, its vision is probably fuzzier than ours. The bouncing rays are brighter, however, so even dim light rays are visible to a cat. The night-prowling house cat seems to have traded off the ability to see a very sharp picture for the ability to see in the dark.

WHY DO CATS GO CRAZY OVER CATNIP?

Catnip contains a chemical that turns on cats. One whiff and cats may roll over and over and rub against the catnip repeatedly. They may also act very excited and playful.

A cat's "catnip fit" is caused by a chemical called *nepetalactone*. This powerful substance is found in tiny glands on the leaves of the herb known as catnip. When the leaves are touched or bruised, small particles, or *molecules*, of nepetalactone are released into the air. Researchers have found that this chemical repels certain leaf-eating insects, providing protection for the plant. Cats, on the other hand, are attracted by nepetalactone. They notice and come around even if there is only a trace of it in the air.

Just as certain drugs mess up the functioning of the human brain, nepetalactone disturbs normal brain activity in many cats. Scientists say that when the chemical is inhaled by cats, it probably acts on the parts of their brain that control behavior and stimulate sexual feelings.

Actually, researchers think nepetalactone is similar to a hormone, or body secretion, that is produced inside female cats to inform their brain that they are ready to mate, or are in *estrus*. This internal secretion affects the brain's behavior control centers, making female cats roll around and act friendly and playful. Male cats don't produce this particular behavior-controlling substance in their bodies.

But both male and female cats playing with catnip may end up with nepetalactone in their brains, and it affects the behavior of both sexes in similar ways. Both exhibit female cat sexual behavior when they are under the influence of this chemical.

It may surprise you to learn that although catnip has a powerful effect on many cats, on others it doesn't work at all. Some cats have brain cells that just don't react to nepetalactone. Whether a cat will go crazy over catnip is determined even before its birth by tiny particles, or *genes*, inherited from its parents.

HOW CAN A CHEETAH RUN SO FAST?

The cheetah is a speed machine. The animal is so fast, in fact, that it can reach speeds of seventy miles per hour for short periods of time. This makes the streamlined predator the fastest runner on earth.

Nearly everything about the cheetah is designed for speed. For example, like most other fast runners, this large cat has specially designed feet. Instead of walking on flat feet like humans, cheetahs walk on their toes. The rest of the cheetah's foot is lengthened and raised off the ground. In this way the length of the foot is added to the length of the leg, making the cheetah's legs very long in relation to the size of its body. These long legs enable the cheetah to take extra big strides to cover more distance with each step.

The cheetah's way of walking isn't as unusual as it may seem. Other fast or moderately fast carnivores, like lions, wolves, dogs, and cats, also walk on their toes. In addition, the speedy *ungulates*, or hoofed mammals, such as horses, deer, and antelope, actually walk on the tips of their hoof-protected toes. On the other hand, slower mammals, such as humans, monkeys, bears, and raccoons, walk on their whole feet, with their toes flat on the ground.

The cheetah also gains speed from its highly moveable shoulder blade, or *scapula*. The shoulder blade is the bone to which a vertebrate's front legs are attached by tough ropelike tissues called ligaments. In the cheetah and other speedy carnivores, the shoulder blade is free to swing back and forth with the leg. In contrast, humans, monkeys, and other slow mammals have shoulder blades that are attached to the collarbone (*clavicle*). These animals can't swing their shoulder blades along with their front limbs. The cheetah's moveable shoulder blade makes its legs longer and its strides bigger.

Additionally, the cheetah gains speed from its flexible spine. A runner's body is actually several inches longer when the back is stretched out, or extended, than when it is bent, or flexed. When the cheetah runs, it constantly flexes and extends its spine. Each time it extends, it adds extra inches to its stride.

Running Cheetah

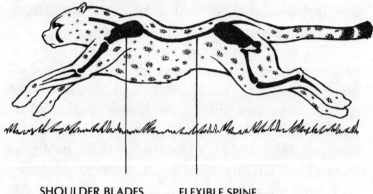

SHOULDER BLADES   FLEXIBLE SPINE

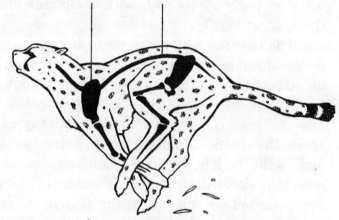

There are many other characteristics that help make the cheetah the world's fastest runner. One feature is the cheetah's sleek, lightweight body, which keeps the animal's muscles from being loaded down. At 130 pounds, the cheetah is actually the lightest of the large African cats. Another feature is the cheetah's long muscular tail. The animal uses this to maintain its balance during high-speed runs.

It is this combination of extra-long strides and a lean, light body that helps to make the cheetah so fast. It uses this speed to overtake prey, such as antelope, as it wanders across the African plains.

WHY DO DOGS PANT?

Dogs pant for the same reason people sweat—to cool their bodies. In both humans and dogs, cooling takes place when moisture evaporates, or passes into the air, from the body's surface. As the moisture gets carried off, it takes heat from the body along with it. This, of course, makes the body temperature drop.

Although the cooling process in both dogs and humans depends mostly on moisture vaporizing in the air, the evaporation occurs in different places. When we humans get overheated, sweat glands all over our body bring fluid and heat from around our blood vessels out to the skin's surface. Then the air moves over the sweat, causing evaporation to occur.

Dogs don't have any sweat glands to bring moisture out to the surface of their skin. Even if they did, the process of evaporation wouldn't work too well. A dog's hairy coat prevents air from circulating freely over the skin, slowing evaporation.

As a result, dogs open their mouths and stick out their long, moist tongues instead! They increase the movement of air over the tongue surface by rapidly drawing breaths in through the nose and forcing them out of the mouth. This is the activity known as panting.

In addition to the evaporative cooling that occurs from the tongue, some cooling also takes place within the length of the dog's nose. A number of tiny sacs, or *glands*, inside the nostrils produce a large quantity of fluid which evaporates as the dog inhales. In a way, these special nasal glands actually serve as sweat glands for the dog.

WHY DO DOGS URINATE ON FIRE HYDRANTS?

When a dog urinates on a fire hydrant it's talking in "smell talk." The smell of the dog's urine is a kind of communication between dogs. Spraying a hydrant or other object is a male dog's way of saying, "I was here, this is my territory."

Although dogs will wet on all sorts of objects, they seem to prefer pole-shaped items such as fire hydrants, tree trunks, and fence posts. Because male dogs lift their legs when they spray, their urine is directed as high off the ground as possible, spreading the scent up into the air.

Not only does a male dog use its urine to advertise its own scent, it also uses it to cover up the scent of a rival. As a dog moves along a street or path, it will sniff at trees and fire hydrants for the scent of others. Dogs seem to be able to sense the difference between male and female dog urine. When a male comes upon another male's urine, it will immediately stop and spray the area with its own scent.

We humans might not think that scent marking is a great way to communicate, but we have a relatively poor sense of smell. Dogs, however, are great smellers. They can smell differences in odors that humans can't detect at all. Urine marking also offers some real advantages to the dog. The animal can mark its territory and then walk away, leaving its message behind. Other dogs will get the message, even though the territory owner isn't there. In addition, the smell of the urine stays around for hours. A dog's mark is a long-lasting signal that remains when the dog moves on to do other things.

Scent marking is such a good way to communicate that its use is fairly widespread among animals. Mammals such as wolves, lions, and cats also use urine to mark their territories. Still others, like rabbits and deer, have special scent glands that they rub on rocks and twigs to give a territorial message.

HOW DO SKUNKS STAND THEIR OWN SMELL?

Skunks always have their own stink bombs with them, but they don't usually stink. Normally, these small mammals keep their special weapon tucked away in two sacs around the tail. As long as the liquid stays in the sacs, skunks don't smell particularly "skunky" to other animals or themselves.

When skunks actually let go with their ammunition, however, the smell is horrible and very strong. Also, if the oily liquid makes contact with the skin and eyes of a human or animal, it causes burning and sometimes temporary blindness.

Moreover, the stink may stay around for days or even weeks.

Apparently skunks don't like this awful smell any more than their victims do. Before releasing a shot, they very carefully lift up their tails so they won't get any of the liquid on themselves. And they make sure to direct the spray away from their own bodies.

In addition, skunks really try to avoid using their weapon. For example, when a threatening-looking individual comes near, skunks don't just swing their rear end around and start spraying. Instead, they attempt to warn off trouble by stamping their feet, stiffening their tails, and perhaps by growling. They fire only if they think they're about to be attacked.

Besides avoiding spraying their awful perfume by stamping and growling, skunks may also ward off enemies with what scientists call *warning coloration*, or their bold black and white markings. This warning coloration is particularly noticeable to other mammals because most mammals are color-blind and see the contrasts of black and white best. (Color-blind animals probably see colors as shades of gray or brown.) After tangling with a skunk only once, most attackers decide to avoid any of these boldly-marked, odor-producing little creatures in the future.

DO BATS REALLY SUCK BLOOD?

Some kinds of bats *do* dine on blood. Called *vampire bats*, these small, winged mammals are the only *vertebrates*, or creatures with backbones, that feed on the blood of other animals. Of the more than eight hundred species of bats in the world, however, only three are vampires. All three kinds live in Central and South America.

The vampire bat takes its meals mainly at night when its victims—usually cows, horses, or chickens—are asleep. After easing onto a host animal's body, the fast-moving little predator uses its needle-sharp front teeth to scrape a shallow wound in the victim's skin. This happens so quickly and efficiently the victim normally doesn't even wake up.

Now the vampire begins feeding, simply lapping up its liquid meal from the cut. The bat's dining process is aided by a special *anticlotting* agent that drips with its saliva into the wound. Normally blood flowing from a cut quickly forms a *clot*, or lumplike plug for the hole, but the anticlotting chemical prevents this from happening to the bat's dinner. Thus, the blood keeps coming and the bat continues to lap it up.

Once a vampire bat has opened a wound, it often keeps feeding for twenty or thirty minutes, until its stomach is completely full. The bat may even consume more than its own body weight in blood and become so heavy it can barely fly!

Despite their gross eating habits, these unattractive, brown-colored creatures are not at all like the terrible "vampire" monsters seen in horror movies. For one thing, vampire bats are only about two and a half to three inches long, small enough to fit in the palm of your hand. Moreover, a vampire bat's bite doesn't normally kill or seriously injure its victim. Even when they gorge themselves, they generally can't take enough blood to weaken the host animal. The real problem is that the bats may carry disease germs in their saliva. These germs can get passed, or transmitted, to a victim when bats feed. For example, in Central and South America vampires have been known to transmit rabies to cattle and other animals.

HOW DO BATS FIND THEIR WAY IN THE DARK?

Even in the darkest cave or blackest night, bats can tell where they're going. That's because they use a remarkable radarlike guidance system to *hear* rather than see their way around.

This system of seeing with sound is called *echolocation*. If you have ever shouted into the distance and then heard an echo, you already know something about how both sound and echolocation work. Normally sound waves travel out through the air until they hit a surface. Then they bounce back toward their source again. It is this special rebounding of sound waves, or echoing, that makes the bats' guidance systems possible.

Of course, in order to have echoing, you've got to have sounds! So a flying bat creates its own sound waves by sending out a series of rapid chirps. Depending on the kind of bat and its particular situation, the chirps may occur from about once a second to ninety or more times a second. Bat chirps cannot usually be heard by humans because these

Bat Using Echolocation

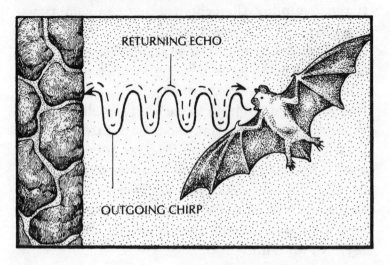

sound waves are too high-pitched, or vibrate too rapidly, for our ears to pick up. The human ear can hear sounds that vibrate, or move back and forth, from twenty to eighteen thousand times a second, and bat chirps vibrate up to ninety thousand times a second.

The bat, however, can not only hear the chirps, but can easily pick up their echoes. Then it immediately uses the echoes to come up with a lot of valuable information. For example, by noting how much time passes between the chirp and the return of its echo, the little mammal can estimate how far away an object is. The farther away something is, the longer it takes for a sound wave bouncing off it to return. By noticing exactly what direction the echo comes from, the bat can tell whether the object its sound waves hit is on the left, on the right, or straight ahead. Since the shape, size, and texture of whatever is hit affect the particular sound of the echo, the bat can sometimes even identify the object and estimate its size.

With such a marvelous signal-sending and echo-monitoring system in operation, bats have no difficulty dodging objects during flight. In fact, since they can locate objects so easily, they also put the system to work hunting food. Bats just send out their chirping signals and then zoom in when the echoes indicate that a juicy insect or other prey is nearby. Their echolocation skills are so incredible that some bats are able to zero in on prey as small as fruit flies and catch up to twelve hundred of them in an hour.

WHY DOES A GORILLA BEAT ITS CHEST?

When a gorilla beats its chest it may look like it's getting ready to attack, but actually this physical display can have a number of different meanings. And although we associate chest beating with enraged adult males, gorillas of both sexes communicate using this behavior. Often they use it just to indicate they're excited, but it can "say" other things depending on the situation.

Sometimes, beating its chest is a gorilla's way of talking tough. When an adult male gorilla senses danger it often rises up on its hind legs, hoots loudly, and pounds its palms (*not* its fists) against its chest. At the same time, it may break off branches, throw objects, pull up grass, and run from side to side. A male is especially likely to talk tough if it heads a family group, or troop, and thus has other gorillas to defend. Scientists call this chest beating show a *threat display*.

While a three-hundred- to four-hundred-pound mature male gorilla can easily overpower most opponents, its chest beating is normally intended to scare off enemies, not start fights. In fact, despite what you may have seen in the movies, scientists say these huge apes are rather shy, gentle creatures and usually prefer to avoid confrontations. Talking tough is a defensive measure to insure they are left alone.

On occasion, these large mammals also use their chests as drums to signal other troop members that are out of sight. This may occur when individuals spread out to feed or rest in thick foliage. By drumming every once in a while, family members can signal their locations and keep from drifting too far apart. In addition, the leader of a troop may call his group back together or alert them to trouble with some loud chest thumps.

Young gorillas occasionally stand on their hind legs and beat their chests, but usually this is done in play. A fierce bout of thumping may serve as a challenge to other youngsters to roughhouse. "I'm big," the young ape seems to announce, "and I bet you can't beat me!" Sometimes, a youngster also thumps its chest to get its mother's attention.

WHY DO WHALES SPOUT?

When a whale spouts, it's like a gigantic balloon letting out air. Actually, spouting is the whale's way of expelling its breath. This giant mammal holds so much air that it may exhale more than five hundred gallons in one whoosh!

A whale's spout usually looks more like a geyser of water or steam than a column of air. This is because the air becomes warm and moist while held in the creature's body. The moisture in this air then *condenses*, or forms droplets, when it contacts the cooler atmosphere outside. This same process of *condensation* occurs when we see our breath in the atmosphere on a cold day.

The reason the whale needs to inhale and exhale such huge quantities is that it is an air-breather faced with the problem of living in the water. Since it can't get its oxygen from water like fish do, it must return to the surface regularly to replenish its oxygen supply. To help keep these trips to a minimum, the whale's body is equipped with a gigantic air storage facility, its chest cavity. Some species of whales can hold so much air that they are able to stay underwater for one and a half to two hours at a time!

Whenever the oxygen supply in the whale's body is used up, the creature quickly rises to the surface to spout out the stale air and grab a fresh breath. The stale air that the whale releases is under great pressure, as a result of the animal's deep-water dive. The pressure develops when the whale moves far under the water, causing the weight of the water above to press down heavily on it. This pressure on the whale causes the stale air inside the animal to compress, or get packed into a small space. When the whale rises quickly to the surface and exhales, the pressure rapidly lessens and the stale air is released in a powerful spout. In some cases the spout can shoot up forty to fifty feet high.

Whales' spouts always emerge from blowholes, one or two small openings on the top of their heads. The blowholes are forced open by the column of air, then automatically close to prevent any water from getting in. It may surprise you to learn that these "head holes" are really the animal's nostrils! Having nose holes where your hat goes might seem ridiculous to us humans, but for a water-living animal that breathes air it is very handy indeed. The whale, the world's largest mammal, is designed so it can come to the surface and take in air without having to lift up its huge head.

WHY DON'T BEAVERS' TEETH WEAR DOWN WHEN THEY GNAW ON TREES?

Beavers' teeth *do* wear down. Nevertheless, these animals don't ever lose their gnawing ability. That's because their large front cutting teeth keep growing all the time. Also, these special teeth, or *incisors*, wear down in a way that actually helps keep them sharp. Here's how it happens.

The fronts of a beaver's four incisors are covered with a super-hard coating of orange-colored enamel. This enamel strengthens the front surface of the teeth, which helps prevent excessive wear. There is no enamel on the backs of the incisors, however. Thus, they are not protected and wear away faster than the fronts.

As you can see from the drawing, the uneven wearing causes the incisors to develop a chisel-like shape. This makes them perfect for biting out chunks of wood. Beavers can sharpen the edges of their teeth even more by scraping the bottom incisors against the upper ones. Armed with such wonderful cutting tools, the beaver has been known to chop through a five-inch-thick tree in less than fifteen minutes.

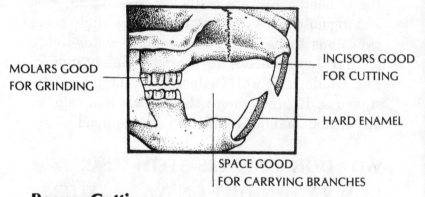

MOLARS GOOD
FOR GRINDING

INCISORS GOOD
FOR CUTTING

HARD ENAMEL

SPACE GOOD
FOR CARRYING BRANCHES

Beaver Cutting Down Tree

Although the incisors are the beavers' only ever-growing choppers, their eight back teeth are also very well designed for their job. Called *molars*, these have much more rounded surfaces and are used for crushing and grinding twigs, bark, and wood chips to a pulp. (The grinding teeth don't need to be ever-growing, because they will still work when worn down.) The molars are set far back in the mouth, leaving a large space between them and the four incisors. This gap is useful too— it provides beavers a good place for gripping and carrying lengths of saplings and small trees in their mouths.

HOW DOES A SQUIRREL FIND BURIED NUTS?

A squirrel can't remember where it's buried nuts, but it still doesn't have much trouble finding them. This bushy-tailed rodent depends on its sense of smell to locate its buried food. A squirrel's sensitive nose can easily pick out the smell of a nut that is buried several inches underground. In fact, the squirrel's sense of smell is so good, it can tell the difference between a good nut and a rotten one. This means it doesn't need to waste its energy cracking open bad nuts.

Not all squirrels are nut buriers. Ground squirrels live in underground burrows. They either store winter food right in their burrows or spend the cold months in *hibernation*, or winter sleep. Tree squirrels, such as red squirrels, gray squirrels, and flying squirrels, on the other hand, are all food buriers. The tree squirrel's ability to bury nuts helps it to survive long, cold winters.

Normally the squirrel begins to "squirrel away" food in autumn. At this time there is usually an abundance of tasty nuts covering the ground. The hungry squirrel stuffs its belly with food and then hides the leftovers under the earth.

Never too fussy about where it places its winter nuts, the tree squirrel often buries them right where it finds them. It can cover up a nut in less than a minute and can bury more than forty nuts in an hour.

Squirrels are not only efficient about burying and finding nuts, but they are also quite skilled at opening them. They make use of their large, sharp front teeth, or incisors, to gnaw through the nut's shell. Like beavers, squirrels have continuously growing incisors with extra-sharp edges (see page 19, "Why Don't Beavers' Teeth Wear Down When They Gnaw on Trees?"). Squirrels use their upper teeth to make a clean slice around the nutshell and their lower teeth to wedge open the hard covering. This may seem like the obvious way to open a nut to us, but squirrels actually must learn how to do it.

Young squirrels begin by gnawing holes all over the nut. With a little bit of practice, however, youngsters quickly become skillful at the job.

DO SHEEP SHIVER AFTER SHEARING?

Yes, newly sheared sheep do shiver if the weather is chilly. After all, these animals don't produce wool so humans can make sweaters. They grow it so they can stay warm in winter. Naturally, when their thick, fuzzy coat is clipped off, sheep feel the cold more and may start shivering to warm up.

The main reason that shearing causes sheep to shiver is that the freshly clipped animals don't have time to adjust to the sudden loss of "clothes." Under natural conditions in the wild, sheep do an excellent job of tolerating a range of temperatures by changing the length and thickness of their fleece. In fall, for example, their coats gradually become heavier, so that by winter many species of sheep have enough protective fleece to live comfortably in temperatures of twenty degrees below zero Fahrenheit. Then, in spring, the furry mammals gradually shed their winter coats and lighter summer ones come in. Sheared domestic sheep, on the other hand, can only feel drafty and wait until their fleece grows back.

Farmers know that newly sheared sheep are susceptible to chilling, so they always do their clipping in spring. In places like the Shetland Islands, where even springs and summers are cold, shearers make a point of leaving at least a thin layer of wool on the animals. This lessens the shock to their bodies and gives the sheep some protection from the cold.

WHY DO COWS CHEW THEIR CUD?

Cows spend so much time chewing cud they even do it in their sleep! However, these animals don't spend long hours chomping just to exercise their jaws. The endless chewing enables them to digest the grass and hay they eat. Extra chewing is necessary to break down a tough substance called *cellulose* found in the cell walls of all plants.

Cellulose digestion is not only difficult for cows, but it creates problems for all vertebrates, or animals with backbones. Vertebrates lack the special chemicals, or *enzymes*, that are necessary to break down the cellulose. *Herbivores*, or plant-eating mammals, do have some wonderful ways of solving this problem, however. These mammals carry a special group of microscopic, cellulose-digesting bacteria right in their digestive tracts. These bacteria break down cellulose, thus providing both themselves and their host animals with nutrients. This living arrangement is called a *symbiotic* relationship, which means that it benefits both the bacteria and their host.

Cows belong to a special group of herbivorous animals called *ruminants*. The ruminants—which also include sheep, goats, giraffes, and deer—are super cellulose eaters. They are all cud-chewing mammals that house their helpful, symbiotic bacteria in a special, greatly enlarged stomach called the *rumen*. Actually, these mammals have four different stomachs, and each one assists in cellulose digestion.

In a cow, cellulose digestion starts when the animal chews and swallows its food. The vegetable matter then moves into the *esophagus*, a long food tube that takes it to the rumen. Here, the food is wetted and churned into a soupy mass. At the same time, bacteria begin to break it down. Next, the

Four-chambered Stomach of a Cow

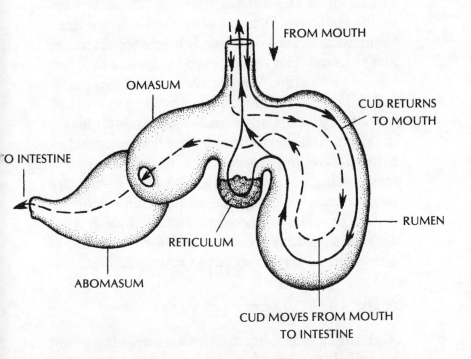

OMASUM

FROM MOUTH

CUD RETURNS TO MOUTH

'O INTESTINE

RETICULUM

ABOMASUM

RUMEN

CUD MOVES FROM MOUTH TO INTESTINE

food moves to the second stomach, or *reticulum*. Inside the reticulum are many small sections, where the food is packed into lumps, or cuds. The cuds are then moved back up to the mouth.

Cud is passed from the stomach to the mouth through the cow's esophagus. Unlike humans, cows and other cud-chewers have special muscles to move material up as well as down the food tube. (You can actually observe these up-and-down movements of cud by watching a cud-chewing giraffe in the zoo. The long neck of a giraffe makes it easy to see a bulge of food pass between the stomach and the mouth.)

After cud reaches the mouth, it is further broken down as the animal chews it. The cow then swallows the cud. This time the food enters a third stomach, called the *omasum*. Here the food is mixed and churned, and then moved to the fourth stomach, or *abomasum*. The abomasum produces chemicals that digest the food even more.

After the partially digested plant matter leaves the stomach it moves into the small intestine. Herbivores have longer intestines than carnivores, or meat-eating animals. This is because plants are much harder to digest than meat and a long intestine provides a large surface for completing the difficult digestion process. The coiled intestine of a cow can be stretched out to reach 165 feet.

WHY ARE GIRAFFES SO TALL?

A giraffe is like a watchtower and warning guard all rolled into one. Using a neck that's up to ten and a half feet long and keen eyesight, the giant animal can peer over the treetops and spot a lion or other predator more than a half mile away. If it is alarmed, the giraffe will snort and run off. This behavior also alerts any other animals in the area. Zebras and other medium-sized prey animals seem to take advantage of the giraffe's super lookout abilities by staying close to giraffe herds.

Not only does the giraffe's long neck help it to spot predators, but its long legs give it the ability to fight them off. If, for example, a lion does sneak up on an unsuspecting giraffe, a few swift kicks from it will usually send the lion reeling.

Being tall also gives giraffes a great advantage at feeding time. The big mammals can easily munch on tree leaves that shorter animals can't reach. Giraffes can also bend their flexible necks and chomp on vegetation from bushes and shrubs.

The ability to feed on tree leaves not only cuts out the competition, it also gives the giraffes another important advantage over grass feeders. Wildebeest, zebras, and other African plains animals that feed on grass face major problems during the dry season. At that time grasses dry up and the shorter herbivores, or plant eaters, must often wander long distances in search of fresh green food. The trees, on the other hand, with thin, deeper roots, may stay leafy through the drought, enabling the giraffes to find all their food without having to wander from place to place.

HOW DO GIRAFFES LIE DOWN?

Lying down is no simple matter when you're eighteen feet tall. So when a giraffe settles down to sleep, it only settles part of the way. The giant animal lies down by tilting its body to one side and stretching one leg out, while tucking its other legs under. If it simply wants to chew its cud, doze, or rest, the giraffe sits with its long neck upright. When it wants to go into deep sleep, it arches its neck backwards and rests its head on the ground near its tail.

A giraffe never lies flat on its side. Like other cud chewers, or ruminants, it must always keep its body in a fairly upright position to help the

Giraffe Sleeping

complex digestive process taking place in its stomach (see "Why Do Cows Chew Their Cud? on page 23 for more information on cud chewing).

Sometimes giraffes actually doze standing up. Often in the afternoon, they will stand with their necks relaxed and dropping downward and their eyelids drooping. Although they aren't as alert as usual, they're probably not actually in deep sleep. Because giraffes sleep with their eyes open, it is difficult to tell if they are actually sleeping deeply. It appears, however, that they do their real sleeping when they are lying down. Even then, they do not sleep for very long. An adult giraffe bends its neck into the sleep position about five times a night, and only keeps it there for around four minutes each time. So it seems to sleep a mere twenty minutes a night! Younger giraffes, however, sleep in more frequent stretches of up to sixty minutes.

When a giraffe is ready to stand up, it faces the difficult problem of lifting its two-thousand-pound body up from the ground. To help do this, the animal makes use of its long, powerful neck. It pulls the neck back and then thrusts it forward to push itself onto its front knees. It then repeats the movement to push its body forward and fully raise its hind legs. A third thrust enables the giraffe to shift its body backwards, straighten its front legs, and stretch to its full seventeen or eighteen feet in height. The whole process requires one and a half seconds. This may not seem like much, but it's too long if there's a hungry lion rushing to attack. This is probably why giraffes only lie down for brief naps. In addition, giraffes will only take their snoozes when other giraffes are nearby to help alert them to danger.

WHY DO ELEPHANTS HAVE TRUNKS?

The elephant has the most useful nose in the animal kingdom. In fact, the elephant's trunk—which actually includes both a nose and lips—is vital for survival. Elephants that have seriously injured or lost their trunks in accidents normally do not live very long.

Although the trunk may not look particularly fancy or complicated to us humans, its design makes it a wonderful all-purpose tool for the elephant. About forty thousand muscles and tendons packed inside give the trunk its strength and flexibility. Its length and rubbery texture enable it to reach quite far in all directions. Nerve hairs scattered on the outside surface give the organ a good sense of touch. Moreover, depending on the kind of elephant, the tip of the trunk contains either one or two fingerlike parts that can pick up even very small objects.

One great advantage of the elephant's trunk is that it helps the gigantic mammal do things its big, cumbersome body couldn't otherwise manage. For example, the elephant can reach out and explore places such as marshes and water holes that wouldn't support its great weight. It can also squeeze its "arm" into tight spots and reach high into trees where its body could never go.

This armlike appendage makes a lot of tasks easier. For instance, the twenty-thousand-pound beast can push and pull objects without going to the trouble of shifting its bulk around. It can search the ground without having to bend down or raise and lower its incredibly heavy head. And of course, it can use the trunk to grasp and pick up food and other things, an important ability very few animals have. (See "Why Do Opossums Hang from Trees by Their Tails?" on page 36 for information on another animal with this rare ability.)

Additionally, the elephant's trunk gives it a keen sense of smell and touch. Elephants are constantly sniffing, feeling, and patting one another. In times of danger, they also wave their superlong noses high to test the air. And when it is angered or alarmed, the beast can send a blast of air out of its trunk that produces a loud trumpeting sound.

Perhaps the niftiest use of the elephant's tubelike trunk is as a hose. The elephant sucks up and sprays out water either for drinking or bathing. To drink, the huge creature simply squirts the water from its trunk into its mouth. To bathe, it lifts its trunk overhead and gives itself a shower. Sometimes it gives itself a powder bath by sucking up dirt with its trunk and blowing it over its body.

WHY DO DEER HAVE ANTLERS?

A male deer's antlers serve as a kind of fancy headpiece, advertising that he is strong and able to fight for a mate. If a male deer, or *buck*, has large antlers, he can often frighten off a smaller rival just by displaying them.

Antlers also work as powerful, piercing weapons when bucks actually go into battle. The fighting males often begin their attacks by charging at each other's sides. As a buck rushes toward his rival, the sharp branches, or *tines*, of his antlers may pierce the opponent's body. Such an injury not only frightens off a rival, but may also lead to his death.

Sometimes, two fighting bucks will butt their antlers against each other and begin a shoving match. In this kind of contest a strong buck will be able to push off a weaker one. Occasionally, however, both fighters end up losing because their horns become locked together and cannot be pulled apart. In this case, the bucks cannot eat or defend themselves from predators, and neither will survive for long.

Although antlers look as if they are permanently attached to a deer's head, they aren't. The hard, bony headpieces are shed every year and replaced by a new set. Each new set is usually bigger and has more branches than the one from the year before. Thus, an old buck will have much more impressive antlers than a young one. The mature, common white-tailed deer may grow antlers that are two and a half feet from tip to tip. A large moose, another kind of deer, may carry a set that stretches six feet across.

Antlers are actually made out of bone that grows from a deer's head. They grow with amazing speed, requiring only six months from start to finish. In North America, deer begin to grow their antlers in March. The growing antlers are covered with a soft skin called *velvet*. When the antlers finally stop growing in August, the velvet peels off, leaving a clean white headpiece. These mature antlers are carried through the fall mating season and on into the winter. They are finally shed in January or February, leaving the deer bareheaded for one or two months. While antlers are commonly found only on the heads of male members of the deer family (Cervidae), the reindeer are an exception. Both males and females of the species carry around large, showy antlers.

WHY DO ZEBRAS HAVE STRIPES?

Strange as it seems, a zebra's flashy coat probably helps it hide from lions and other predators. The bold black-and-white stripes that cover a zebra's body actually make the animal look less like a zebra. These stripes break up the outline of the

animal, an effect known as *disruptive coloration*. This means that to a hungry lion, a distant herd of zebras can look like a confusing mass of stripes, rather than a tasty group of animals. The lion's confusion may be increased by waves of heat that often rise in a shimmering haze over the hot African plains where zebras live.

A zebra's stripes are more effective because they run vertically, or up and down. To understand why this is true, examine the drawing. Now place this book on the other side of the room and look at it again. What did you see? The zebra with the vertical stripes will blend into the background, while the zebra with the horizontal stripes stands out clearly. The vertical stripes break up the shape of the zebra into a series of long white boxes. The horizontal stripes follow the horselike shape of the zebra and emphasize it.

WHY DOES A CAMEL HAVE A HUMP?

Camels' humps are fat packs that help them stay cool. Although some people think these large bulges are filled with water, they actually contain fat, up to one hundred pounds of it! In the desert-living dromedary camel, this fat is packed tightly into a single stiff hump. In the cold-loving Bactrian camel, the fat is stuffed into two squishy humps. The packed fat serves both as a barrier against heat and an extra energy supply.

In times of plenty, a camel's body stores extra food energy in its hump in the form of fat. When food supplies get low, the camel uses this extra fat to survive. As the camel lives off its fat, its hump or humps shrink. In Bactrian camels, the soft, shrunken twin humps often flop over to one side.

Actually, it's not unusual for an animal to store its extra food energy as fat. Most animals, however, tend to have their fat spread around their body, particularly around the belly. Camels, on the other hand, pack all their fat into one or two lumps on the back. This strange way of storing fat makes it easier for the camel to stay cool in the desert. Fat is a good insulator. It works like a wall to keep the heat inside an animal's body from getting out and the heat outside an animal's body from getting in. When the hot sun beats down on the camel's back, the hump prevents some of the heat from passing into the camel's body.

The hump's heat-blocking abilities are improved by the camel's thick wool coat. Not only does it help keep out the heat, but the coat's pale color reflects the sun's rays, causing them to bounce off its skin instead of being absorbed.

Even with its heat-blocking hump and skin, a camel can become fairly warm on a hot desert day. Its body temperature can rise to around 104 degrees in the daytime. Unlike humans and most other nondesert mammals, the camel is not hurt by such a temperature change. The humped mammal can comfortably hold this heat until night. Then heat readily leaves the camel through its thin, fatless belly skin and the camel's body temperature may drop to as low as 93.2 degrees.

WHY DO OPOSSUMS HANG FROM TREES BY THEIR TAILS?

An opossum has a tail designed to give it a hand! This small, furry mammal's tail is actually used as a hand to grasp and hold things. Scientists call a tail or other body part that is able to grasp and pick up things *prehensile*. (See "Why Do Elephants Have Trunks?" on page 29 for information on another body part that is prehensile.)

A prehensile tail is especially handy to the opossum because this creature is *arboreal*, meaning that it spends a lot of time in trees. While climbing from branch to branch, the cat-sized mammal uses its tail as a security rope to help keep from falling. Its tail also serves as an extra "hand," when the opossum wants to free its paws for other tasks. Monkeys, which are also arboreal animals, often use their tails in the same way.

You may have seen drawings of opossums simply resting as they dangle by their tails from a limb, but researchers say such pictures aren't really accurate. Usually, these mammals hold on not only with their tails, but with at least one of their long-toed, handlike paws as well. In addition, opossums don't generally just hang there for no reason. As its tail and a foot or two hold the animal fast to the branch, the free "hands" are usually busy with chores such as eating, washing, or grooming its young. Opossums also use the hanging posture to dangle from high, thin branches and gain access to fruits and other foods that most animals can't reach.

Although opossums most frequently depend on their prehensile tail for climbing tasks, this convenient body part is often put to work carrying things as well. Opossums have been seen gathering up bundles of leaves and other nest-making materials with their front feet, then gripping them with their tails to tote them home.

WHAT'S IT LIKE
INSIDE A KANGAROO'S POUCH?

A kangaroo's pouch is more than a baby carrier. It's a cozy home with a built-in feeding machine. Inside the warm, dark pouch are four *teats*, or nipples. These are like soft straws that supply milk when a young kangaroo suckles. The rest of the pouch is empty, leaving lots of space for a young kangaroo to grow.

A baby kangaroo, or *joey*, is born after only thirty-three days inside its mother's womb. The newborn joey looks as if it's come out of its mother too soon. It is only the size of a lima bean, blind, furless, and almost completely helpless. In addition, the little creatuxre is very unkangaroolike. It has tiny bumps where its huge hind legs will eventually grow. Its front legs, on the other hand, which will be rather small and spindly in adulthood, are fairly large.

Soon after birth, the little kangaroo uses its well-developed front legs to pull itself up the fur on its mother's belly and into her pouch. As the struggling newborn inches its way up into the pouch, the mother kangaroo offers no assistance. Amaz-

Kangaroo Nursing Two Joeys

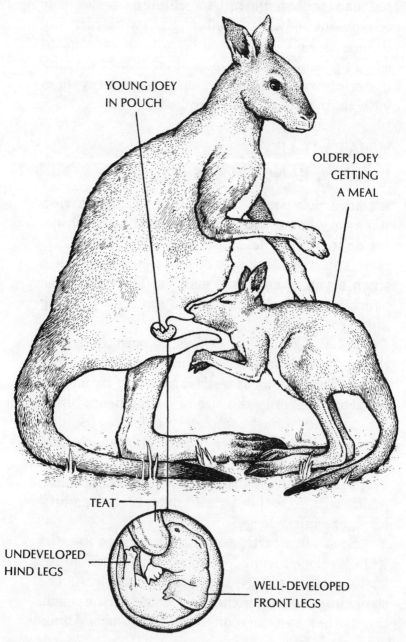

YOUNG JOEY
IN POUCH

OLDER JOEY
GETTING
A MEAL

TEAT

UNDEVELOPED
HIND LEGS

WELL-DEVELOPED
FRONT LEGS

ingly, the sightless little youngster finds her pouch using only its keen sense of smell.

Once inside the warm pouch, the joey catches onto one of its mother's teats. The teat swells in the joey's mouth, enabling the young kangaroo to stay firmly attached to its food tube. As the joey grows, so does the teat. By the time the young kangaroo leaves the pouch the teat will have stretched to four inches in length.

A joey remains totally hidden in its mother's dark pouch during the early months of its life. In one species, called the red kangaroo, the joey does not poke its head out of the pouch and get a glimpse of the world until it is five months old.

As a young kangaroo grows, it also gains weight. A medium-sized joey weighing as much as twenty pounds is still carried around by its mother. The tough elastic walls of the pouch make it possible for the mother to carry her ever-growing load.

A young red kangaroo first leaves its mother's pouch at about six months of age. At this time it begins to wander about, bask in the sun, and graze on grass. The joey, however, continues to return to the pouch for milk and safety.

After the joey has reached eight months of age, it leaves the pouch for good. At this time, the mother kangaroo often gives birth to a second joey. The older joey is too big to get back into the pouch without crushing the baby. It can, however, continue to stick its head into the pouch and suckle. The newborn attaches to a different teat inside the pouch. Each joey continues to suckle on the same teat throughout its nursing period.

What's It Like Inside a Kangaroo's Pouch? **39**

As a joey grows, the milk produced by the teat it suckles changes. At first, a thin watery fluid comes out of the teat. As the newborn gets older, a richer milk is produced. When a mature joey stops nursing, the elongated teat it used stops releasing rich milk and shrinks back to a small size so that it is ready for another newborn. This ability to make two kinds of milk at the same time is an amazing feature of a kangaroo's mammary glands. In this way, the female kangaroo's milk-making apparatus is designed to accommodate two different-aged joeys at once.

IS A PLATYPUS REAL?

Pretend you're creating a very weird animal by mixing parts of mammals, birds, and reptiles. Start with a furry, rodent-shaped body and attach four webbed feet. Add a ducklike bill and a flat, beaverlike tail. Have the creature lay leathery eggs like a reptile, but let the young drink their mother's milk like baby mammals do.

Maybe it's hard to believe, but your crazy creation is a real live animal known as the platypus. This shy, rarely seen creature is found only along the coast of Australia and neighboring regions. Since it spends most of its time in the water and in burrows along riverbanks, researchers still don't know a lot about its habits. They do know that the platypus uses its strange webbed feet for paddling and its soft, rubbery bill to catch tadpoles, shrimp, worms, and other small water animals for dinner.

Platypus

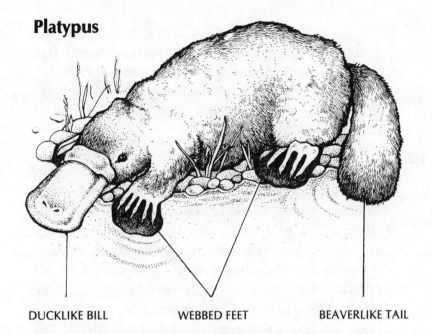

DUCKLIKE BILL   WEBBED FEET   BEAVERLIKE TAIL

Experts also know that mother platypuses prepare nests and *incubate*, or warm, their eggs with their large flat tails and furry abdomens for about two weeks until the young hatch. Platypus eggs are less than an inch in diameter, and the just-hatched babies are even smaller, about a half-inch long. At first, they don't have hair and can't see and stay nestled against their mother's abdomen. Then, after a week, her underbelly begins to ooze milk and the young start to feed by lapping it up. Gradually, over a six-week nursing period, the babies begin to mature and look like their parents.

The platypus is so strange that for many years scientists had trouble believing it was real. The problem was the platypus didn't quite fit into the biologists' existing animal family groups. Scientists had already determined that, among other things, mammals have fur and produce milk for their young. Yet, while the platypus clearly has these characteristics, it also produces rubbery, reptilelike eggs and then incubates, or warms them, the way birds and some reptiles do. So, what kind of animal is it?

Eventually, researchers decided that the platypus really is a mammal, but that it belongs in a special mammal category called *monotremes*. There are only a few species of monotremes, including the platypus and several types of spiny anteaters. All the monotremes are found in Australia and neighboring areas. *Taxonomists*, or scientists who group animals into categories, say monotremes probably didn't come from the same large evolutionary group as other mammals. Instead, they came from a small side group and developed unique characteristics all their own.

WHY DO BIRDS HAVE FEATHERS?

A bird's feathers form the ultimate coat. They're extra warm and yet very light in weight. They keep a bird toasty without making it so heavy that it can't get off the ground.

Warm feathers are important to birds. They enable the small creatures to speed through the air without getting chilled. They also make it possible for birds to live in extra-cold places like the Arctic.

You may wonder how such lightweight things as feathers can provide so much warmth. The secret lies in the feather's design. It is thin and fluffy and can trap a layer of air against the bird's skin. It is this layer of air that helps to keep the bird warm. If a bird is cold, it can raise or fluff up its feathers. Fluffing them enables the feathers to trap a thicker layer of air, which provides more insulation for the bird. People make use of the warming qualities of fluffy down feathers in their jackets and quilts.

In addition to providing warmth, a bird's feathers are specially designed to assist in flight. They cover the bird with a smooth, streamlined surface, which helps it glide through the air at speeds that bats could never reach. Feathers also assist flight in another way. Special parts called *barbs* make a bird's wing strokes more efficient. Barbs are the thin, hairlike structures that stick out from either side of the long, tube-shaped shaft of the feather. Here's how the barbs on feathers work.

Each barb is equipped with very tiny hooklets, which link all the barbs together when they are pushed upward, and unhook when the barbs are pushed down. You can watch them work for yourself, if you try this little experiment. Hold a feather in your hand and stroke the barbs upward. You will see that they form a nice smooth surface, or vane. If you stroke the barbs downwards, they will separate into thin, wispy strands.

The operation of the hooklets can be seen when a bird is in flight. A flying bird generally has two kinds of wing strokes, a downstroke and an upstroke. On the downward stroke, the bird uses its wings to push against the air. This moves the bird forward, in much the same way that putting a boat's oar into the water and pulling backwards will move a boat forward. As the bird strokes its wings down, the barb's hooklets close. The bird's wings present a smooth unbroken surface to the air. On the upstroke, which is usually a recovery stroke, the hooklets on the feathers unhook. The barbs separate, and air can rush through the wing, rather than pushing against it.

In between wing strokes, birds often glide. To do this, a bird folds up its wings and makes its body as small and streamlined as possible. (When

The Structure of a Bird's Feather

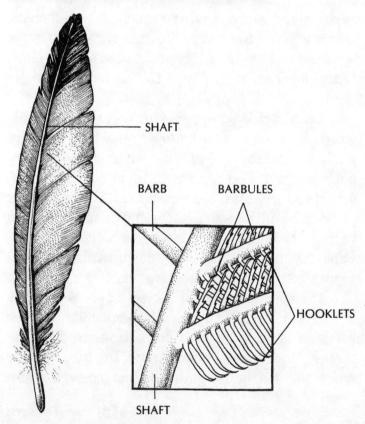

SHAFT

BARB   BARBULES

HOOKLETS

SHAFT

a bird glides on currents of air, however, it keeps its wings opened so they can catch the wind. See "How Do Birds Soar in Circles?" on page 54 for more information on wind gliding.) A bird's marvelous feathers are designed so that they fit neatly over one another and thus allow the bird to fold its wings.

WHY DON'T DUCKS GET SOAKED IN THE WATER?

Just as shingles form a protective waterproof covering for a house, feathers provide a protective covering for a duck. Like shingles, feathers fit together in neat, overlapping rows. This design encourages water to run off instead of staying and soaking in.

Actually, feathers work even better than shingles because they not only keep water off, but they help a duck to float. A duck can adjust, or fluff, its feathers to trap layers of air next to its skin. These air pockets then act like swimmer inner tubes.

Along with its feathers, a duck also depends on a greasy substance called *preen oil* to keep itself waterproof. The oil is furnished by the duck's preen gland, a small sac at the base of its tail. Until recently, scientists thought that preen oil was the main reason ducks didn't get soaked. They speculated that since water doesn't mix with oil, this oily subtance probably acted as a shield that prevented water from sinking in.

Although preen oil may indeed help block out water, experts now realize it also aids a duck in another way. It works as a grooming oil to keep the duck's water-resistant covering in top condition.

Ducks maintain their plumage in an elaborate grooming activity called *preening*. If you have ever watched ducks after they have been swimming, you've probably seen them preen. First, they rub their bills against the preen gland to pick up some oil. Then, the ducks very carefully go over each of their feathers with their beaks. Sometimes, they use a nibbling, picking, or rubbing motion, and other times they draw the entire length of the feather neatly through their bills. The entire process is designed to clean, oil, and comb their plumage, as well as to straighten any hairlike barbs that are out of place. When they are finished, they shake out, or *rouse*, so the feathers can trap a layer of air and fall neatly back into line.

Ducks instinctively preen themselves after each swim. They know they must put their feathers back in order and replace the oil that washed off. Otherwise, their protective coat might become dry and ruffled and allow water to sink in.

Although preening is especially important to ducks and other waterfowl, all birds spend some time keeping their feathers clean and sleek. This not only helps make their coat rainproof, but provides the streamlined surface that aids flight (see "Why Do Birds Have Feathers?" on page 42).

HOW DO BIRDS FLY?

A bird is a lightweight, streamlined, power pack. Everything about a bird is designed to reduce weight and increase streamlining (smoothing and thinning of the body). It is this combination that makes it possible for these creatures to fly.

Let's examine how a bird accomplishes this remarkable feat. The first thing a bird needs is some force that will lift it off the ground. Amazingly, the force the bird uses is a combination of its own energy and just plain air. Air has weight. At sea level on earth air pushes equally in every direction, both above and below the bird. If, however, the air underneath the bird can be made to push harder than the air above the bird, the air below will push the animal upward. The bird's wings are designed to make air move in just this way.

A bird's wings are rounded in the front, and thin and flat in the back. The wings also are curved upward on the underside, so that the whole wing is shaped like a teardrop.

This teardrop shape affects the way air passes over the wing. As a bird moves forward to take off, air rushes over the wing. Air traveling across the top of the wing hits the front part of the curve and bounces away from the back part. Because of this, there is very little air pressing on the back part of the wing. This means that the air pressure in this spot is low. When air flows across the bottom of the wing, however, it moves more smoothly. The air below the wing therefore has greater pressure than the air above. The greater air pressure on the bottom of the wing pushes the wing upward, creating lift.

Besides specially shaped wings, however, a

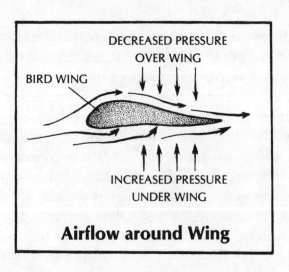

Airflow around Wing

bird must also have the strength and energy to be able to flap its wings and push itself through the air. The bird gets its strength from very powerful wing muscles. It gets its energy from eating high-calorie foods like seeds, worms, insects, and fruits.

Even with its strength and energy, a bird would have a difficult time getting a heavy body off the ground. You might think that a bigger, heavier animal would have more strength than a small one, and, thus, would be a better flier. But the fact is, a small animal has more power per pound than a big one does. Thus, while a mouse is weaker than a man, four thousand mice (which weigh about as much as one man) together have nine times more power. A large, heavy bird has less power per pound than a small one and has a harder time getting airborne.

Since being heavy makes getting airborne more difficult, birds are designed to be as lightweight as possible. For one thing, a bird's bones are thin and hollow instead of being thick and filled with marrow like ours. Also, unlike other vertebrates, or animals with backbones, birds lack a urinary bladder and thus don't store supplies of heavy urine. Instead, they excrete it in the form of a thick white paste as soon as it's formed.

Feathers are another important feature that helps keep a bird's weight down. Feathers provide a lot of warmth but are much lighter than a mammal's hair (see "Why Do Birds Have Feathers?" on page 42).

Birds also have more streamlined organs for producing young than most other animals. While all other vertebrate females have two egg makers, or ovaries, and two tubes, or oviducts, for transporting them, birds have only one of each. The male bird also has sperm-making testes that shrivel up during most of the year, and only become large during the breeding season.

In addition, birds' heads are not weighted down with heavy teeth. Instead, they have a special muscular pouch in front of their stomachs called the gizzard. Birds swallow small stones and store them in their gizzards to grind up food there. This places weight in the center of the bird's body instead of in its head. Weight in the head would make the bird top-heavy and it would have a hard time maintaining its balance during flight.

All of these important features result in an animal that is extremely lightweight and whose weight is distributed for good balance. The average bird weighs only a few ounces to a few pounds. The heaviest flying bird is the great bustard, a vulture that weighs thirty-one pounds. Bigger, heavier birds, such as ostriches, have completely lost their ability to fly.

WHY DO GEESE FLY IN A V?

Flying in a V with the leader at the point helps geese move through the air with speed and ease. The main reason is that each bird in the V formation helps lift the one behind it. To really understand why this is true, you need to know a little about *bird aerodynamics,* or the way air flows and presses against a flying bird.

When a bird flies, it meets *resistance,* or pressure, from the air. Air doesn't just flow smoothly around a bird and then close up right behind it. Instead, the air hits the thick fronts of the flier's wings and then bounces away, forming a space along the wings' upper surfaces and undersides, as shown in the drawing. In this space, there is now less air to create pressure and push against the wings.

Actually, however, the pressure is not lowered evenly over both sides, and this is one key to a bird's ability to fly. Due to the special shape of birds' wings (see "How Do Birds Fly?" on page 46 for details), more air is actually cleared away from their upper sides than from their undersides. Thus, the pressure actually drops more on the upper sides of the wings. With more pressure now pushing from underneath, the air flowing across the undersides of the wings lifts the bird. Finally, when the upward-pushing air reaches the edges of

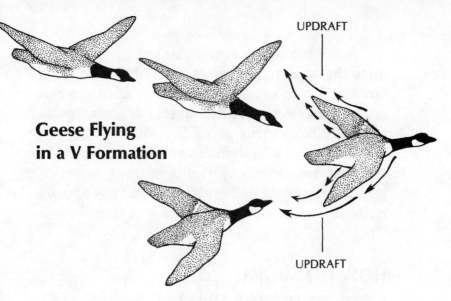

Geese Flying in a V Formation

UPDRAFT

UPDRAFT

the feathers, it rounds the wingtips and rises in a spiral.

The upward spiral of air, or *updraft*, off the wingtips provides lifting power. This is the main reason geese fly in a V. Flock members carefully position themselves behind and to the side of the goose just ahead so that they can catch an updraft and use its lift. This lifting power works against the downward pull of gravity, making it easier for the geese to fly.

There are also some other advantages of the V formation. A flying bird stirs the air behind it, or makes it *turbulent*. Flying directly behind another bird would be like swimming in the bubbly, stirred-up water right behind a motor boat. Flying just to the side of the bird, however, allows the follower to avoid this turbulence and still catch the lift. The angled, spaced lines of the V also give each goose a clear view of the sky ahead and plenty of room to flap its wings.

Since the goose at the point of the V doesn't have the opportunity to catch any lift from other birds, it has to expend more energy than the rest of the flock. As a result, several different geese normally take turns going first during long migratory journeys. Both males and females may take the lead. Regardless of who is in front, however, geese are impressive fliers and can go forty or more miles an hour for several hours at a time.

HOW DO MIGRATING BIRDS FIND THEIR WAY?

Every spring and fall, millions of birds take off on a trip known as migration. For centuries, the mystery of how they find their way has intrigued scientists. We don't have all the answers yet, but we've learned that the process is very complicated. Different kinds of birds use different techniques to get where they want to go. Also, some species have more advanced skills than other species do.

Although some birds journey for days and cross over continents and oceans, not all varieties take such taxing trips. Researchers have discovered that some species go only a few hundred miles and migrate only in daylight when they can see landmarks below them. Apparently these feathered travelers are guided by familiar land forms such as mountain ranges, large lakes, coastlines, and the edges of deserts. When they get close to their destination they then zero in further by using local landmarks like towns, creeks, and fields. This is the simplest method birds use to find their way; it's called *landmark orientation*.

Landmark orientation doesn't work for all birds, or in all situations. Young birds that don't travel with their parents and are migrating for the first time can't look for familiar landmarks because they've never seen the route before. Fliers crossing oceans can't use this method either, because there aren't any landmarks at sea. Such travelers often get their bearings by using the sun as a compass. Amazing as it seems, birds appear to have an inborn mechanism that automatically tells them whether the sun is in the east, south, west, or north at any time of the day. The feathered migrants can then set their own course by flying at the desired angle to the sun.

You might think that finding the way would be trickier in the dark than in daylight, but the majority of migrating birds do travel at night. Many species of night fliers get their bearings from the stars. In fact, scientists have discovered that birds use constellations like the Big and Little Dipper in about the same way human sailors once did. The technique is called *stellar orientation*. Birds that use this method seem to be born with a "star map" in their brain and set their course based on the position of certain star groups in the northern sky. By testing certain birds' reactions to various star patterns in planetariums, scientists have learned that the fliers can use any number of constellations as guides. This means they can keep on track even when clouds cover part of the sky.

Ornithologists, or scientists who study birds,

know there are still other orientation methods, but it isn't clear how all the techniques work. For example, while one kind of European robin migrates at night, researchers have proven it doesn't always get its bearings from stars, or even from moonlight. In fact, when this bird was put in a completely dark wooden container, it was still able to head in the right direction. When it was placed in a heavy steel container, however, the robin couldn't orient itself any more. As a result, experts suspect that the bird may depend on radiation waves, which are blocked out by heavy metal.

Still another method of orienting is used by certain geese. Some species may actually be able to feel the directional pull of the earth's magnetic field and use their own bodies as compasses!

There are still many unanswered questions about the amazing phenomenon of migration. Scientists are continuing their research, but for now the birds are the only ones with all the answers.

HOW DO BIRDS SOAR IN CIRCLES?

Hawks, vultures, and storks are some of the best gliders of the bird world. They hitch a ride on a current of air and glide for hours without flapping their wings. The large birds take advantage of the fact that masses of air often flow upward, creating a force called *lift*. Lift, which acts as a kind of escalator to the clouds, comes in several different forms. Birds rely primarily on a force called *thermal lift*. This occurs as a result of changes in air temperature.

A thermal is a tower of rising air that spirals up from the ground in tight circles. At the top of the tower is a doughnut-shaped mass of circulating air. This doughnut-topped tower forms when the sun beats down on a field. When the air on the field gets warm, it starts to rise in the spiral shape of a thermal. As long as the sun shines, heated air will rise continuously. Thus, thermals form throughout the day and are strongest in the heat of the afternoon.

The upward movement of warm air is not as strange as it may seem. Heated air always rises.

Bird Soaring on a Thermal

That's one reason why the top floor of a house tends to be the warmest. Warm air rises because heat makes the molecules of gas that form the air more energetic and spread out. As it spreads, the warm air rises over the cool, dense air above it.

Thermals first begin to form with the rising of the sun. Some birds can catch a ride on these early weak thermals, but many wait till the sun gets hot and the thermals become stronger. Then the gliders can soar in the air for hours while searching the ground for food.

When the sun sinks in the evening, the air on the ground gets cool and stops forming thermals. Because there are no thermals after sunset, vultures and other soarers glide only during the day. The heavy birds are too big to stay airborne for long without some assistance.

Soaring gives a bird a real advantage in locating a meal. As it soars overhead, a hawk has a great view of the land below and can easily notice if there is a mouse or other potential victim moving about. If a hungry, soaring vulture spots a dead animal, it can move directly to the ground in minutes, beating slower competitors like hyenas, who must move over hills and long stretches of ground to reach a kill. Soarers can also fly long distances, moving from thermal to thermal by spiraling up one and then gliding down to another.

You may wonder why small birds don't take advantage of the thermals the way big ones do. The reason is that a bird usually needs to have large, broad wings to ride on them. The large vultures, hawks, storks, and pelicans are particularly well designed for soaring. Smaller birds with more pointed wings, like gulls and falcons, can only catch a thermal when the winds are strong. If a really strong thermal rises up, however, any bird can get lifted to the sky.

HOW DO VULTURES FIND THEIR FOOD?

When you see a group of vultures circling in the sky, odds are good that there's something dead on the ground. Vultures depend mainly on their excellent vision and soaring abilities to locate their meals.

Vultures are large, odd-looking birds that circle in the skies for hours in search of the dead animals, or carrion, on which they feed (see "How Do Birds Soar in Circles?" on page 54). They are aided in this search by their superior eyesight. It has been estimated that some species of vultures can see eight times better than humans can. In fact, these amazing birds can glide two hundred to three hundred feet up in the air and still locate dead animals on the ground below.

Even with good eyesight, spotting something that isn't moving is not such an easy task. So many species of vultures have found a simpler way to do the job. Instead of looking for carrion, they look for other animals that eat carrion. For example, some species of vultures follow other species of vultures to the site of a kill. Some vultures also search for packs of hyenas as they soar. The carrion-eating hyenas locate their food by smell.

The vultures can simply watch where the hyenas are heading and then use their gliding abilities to get to the carcass first.

Certain species, such as turkey vultures, also use their sense of smell to locate food. Since carcasses are almost always rotted and smelly, you might think that all vultures would use smell to pick out dead meat. Surprisingly, however, some species are not very good smellers. For example, the black vulture has such a poor sense of smell that it will totally ignore a sack of dead meat placed right under its nest. If it can't see the meat, it won't know it's there! Normally, though, the black vulture does just fine, either using its own eyes or following the turkey vulture around.

WHY DO OWLS HUNT AT NIGHT?

It makes sense to go shopping for food when you don't have to battle the crowds. The owl is like a wise shopper; most owls come out at night when hawks and other predatory birds have gone to sleep. At those hours, it doesn't have to compete with other large *carnivorous*, or meat-eating, birds for its meals.

There's another reason why nighttime is a good time for the owl to hunt. Many of the animals that are an owl's food, amphibians, reptiles, and small mammals, share the owl's *nocturnal*, or night-living, habits.

Capturing small, quick-moving creatures in the darkness is not easy, yet owls are extraordinarily good at it. The skilled night hunters rely on their keen senses to make a catch. It might surprise you to learn that one important sense for these birds is vision. Though we humans find it difficult to spot things in poor light, owls have eyes that are specially designed for seeing in the dark.

One reason the owl sees so well at night is because of special eye parts called *rod cells*. These cells sense dim light. Though humans and other diurnal, or daytime, animals also have rod cells, owls have far more, giving them their superior night vision. Owls also have the daylight and color sensitive *cone cells* that are abundant in diurnal species. This means that owls see well in the daytime, too.

The owl's sharp eyesight also results partly from the fact that its eyes are close together on the front of its face. This arrangement means that while the owl's right eye sees a bit more on the right and the left eye a bit more on the left, each one sees nearly the same thing in the middle. When both eyes view the same object, the object is seen as having depth as well as length and height. Owls are similar to humans in having good depth vision, or *depth perception*.

Most birds' eyes are placed on either side of the head. In this case, the right eye sees everything on the bird's right side, while the left eye sees everything on the bird's left side. There is, however, only a small area just in front of the head where both eyes see the same thing. And most birds differ from owls in that they have only this little space where they have depth perception. Most of what they see looks flat.

Why Do Owls Hunt at Night?   **59**

The owl's front-facing eyes help it to spot tiny, moving animals with ease, but they also have a disadvantage. Other birds with their eyes on the sides of their heads can see nearly all the way around behind them. Owls can only see things just a bit on each side. We humans deal with this problem, in part, by using thick muscles to move our eyes around in their sockets. An owl cannot move its eyes, but it does have an incredibly twistable neck. It can keep turning its mobile head in either direction till it faces backwards. In this way the sharp-sighted predator can actually look behind itself, something no other animal can do.

While vision is important for the owl, it is hearing that truly sets it apart from other hunters. For example, a barn owl can use its hearing to locate a field mouse in nearly complete darkness. The nocturnal bird uses its sensitive ears to figure out where the mouse is. If sounds are louder in the owl's left ear than they are in the right ear, then it knows the mouse is on the left. If the sounds are louder in the right ear, then the mouse is on the right. Although some other animals use this same method to determine where objects are, owls are extra good at it.

Many owls have an additional feature that aids their hearing. Their ears are placed unevenly on their heads. In species such as the barn owl, the right ear opens in a tuft of feathers that points upward, while the left ear opens in a tuft of feathers that points down. Each tuft acts like a funnel, catching and directing sound waves into the ear. If sounds are above the owl they're caught first by

Owl with Head Turned Backward

RIGHT EAR OPENING

LEFT EAR OPENING

FACIAL RUFF

the upward tufts of the right ear. If sounds are below the owl, they are captured first by the downward tuft of the left ear. Thus, depending on which ear picks up the sound first, the owl can precisely determine the position of its prey above or below it. This is something that is difficult for other predators to do.

All of these features are special enough, but the owl has still one more. Its excellent hearing is made even better by a special ring of feathers, or ruff, around its face. The facial ruff is made of stiff feathers that catch and amplify sound waves that hit the owl's face. The ruff works for the owl much the way cupping your hand around the back of your ear would work for you.

WHAT DOES A PELICAN DO WITH ITS POUCH?

A pelican's pouch is the perfect portable feeding tool. The fish-eating bird's pouch is a strong, stretchy bag, which can be used as a scoop for gathering up a beakful of squirming seafood. Best of all, the well-designed pouch folds itself up when not in use.

The pelican's amazing fishing gear goes into action when the bird plunges its bill underwater. As the heavy water pours in, the pouch stretches. The enlarged pouch can be swept through the water, enabling the pelican to capture its meal. One species, the brown pelican, has a pouch that can hold more than two gallons of water and hundreds of small fish!

When its pouch is full, a pelican pulls its head up into the air. Out of the water, a full pouch is a very heavy load. The pelican, however, doesn't carry such a load for long. The elastic pouch quickly springs back to its small size, squeezing out water, and leaving the fish behind.

Once it has bagged a meal and drained off the water, the pelican swallows its catch quickly. The large bird would become unbalanced if it had to carry around a pouch full of fish. Its head end would be heavier than its tail end and this would make it difficult for the pelican to get itself airborne. With the fish in its belly, however, the pelican has the added weight near the center of its body. This makes it well balanced and ready for flight.

WHY DOESN'T A SLEEPING BIRD FALL OFF ITS PERCH?

A sleeping bird doesn't fall off its perch because its feet work like handcuffs to lock it on. In fact, the toes and *talons*, or nails, automatically close up around the perch when a bird squats down to sleep and won't unlock again until it stands back up. Here's how the "footcuffs" work.

In the upper part of a bird's leg there are muscles that connect to *tendons*. Tendons are stringlike strips of tissue that run all the way down to the creature's toes. When the bird is standing, its muscles don't pull much on these stringlike strips. The tendons are relaxed and the bird's toes are spread out.

However, when a bird settles down to rest, its bending "knees" tighten the muscles, which in turn pull hard on the tendons. As these are pulled taut, they draw in the bird's toes, automatically curling them around the roost. The feet stay firmly "cuffed" to the perch until the bird rouses itself and wants to stand up.

Birds' Toe-Locking

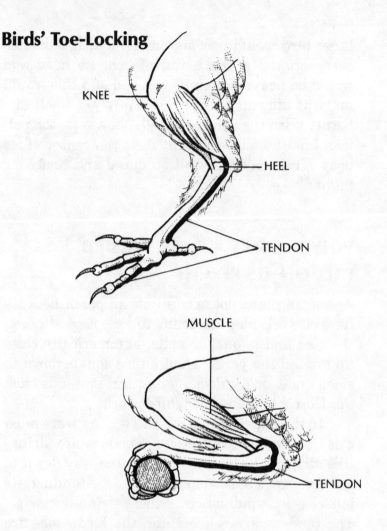

KNEE

HEEL

TENDON

MUSCLE

TENDON

The handy bending and locking process isn't complicated, but it's difficult for us to see because a bird's "knees" are out of sight under its feathers. Though it appears otherwise, the only parts of most birds' legs that are actually visible are their long, scaly feet. As the picture shows, the parts that look like knees bending backwards are actually the creature's heels.

DO BIRDS SING BECAUSE THEY'RE HAPPY?

Nobody knows how birds feel while singing, although they certainly may like to sing. What scientists do know is that singing is a very important means of communication for some kinds of birds.

A bird's song is a special pattern of musical notes or sounds. Typically, a song has a particular rhythm and the notes are always arranged in the same order. For example, a robin's song sounds like "Cheer up, cheerilee! Cheer up, cheerilee!" Some bird songs are more complicated and melodious than the robin's, and others are a bit simpler and less musical. Nevertheless, one or two whistles, squawks, peeps, or other noises do not usually qualify as a song.

In many species of birds, the males do most or all of the singing, and the songsters are likely to sing more during their breeding season. A bird's song seems to say, "I am a male of your species. I have claimed this territory and plan to raise a family here. If you are a female, I invite you to my area. Come share the food on my land and be my mate. If you are a male, stay out. I will defend my territory and chase you off."

Females hearing such songs by males of their species select from among the offers and eventually join a male to mate and nest. Scientists have discovered that females tend to select males that spend the most time singing. Maybe this is because all that tweeting simply attracts their attention. But researchers have found that when a male sings a lot it usually means there's plenty of food in his area. He can spend a lot of time singing simply because he doesn't have to concentrate too much on hunting food. Thus, by choosing the males that sing the most, females are actually improving the chances that they and their young will have plenty to eat.

In some species, both partners of a mated pair sing throughout the breeding season. Scientists think this may help maintain or strengthen the relationship, or the *pair bond*, between the two birds.

Although it might seem as though most birds sing, in actuality only about half of the eighty-five hundred species do. The songsters belong mainly to a group called the *oscines*. This group includes warblers, larks, wrens, mockers, sparrows, and many other familiar songbirds.

WHY ARE MALE BIRDS MORE COLORFUL THAN FEMALES?

It's dangerous for a bird to be pretty! Beautifully colored male birds are easily spotted by sharp-eyed predators. Dull-brown females, on the other hand, can stay well hidden from hungry enemies. Their drab coats enable them to blend in with brown limbs of trees and bushes around them.

If it's so dangerous to be beautiful, you may ask, just why are many male birds so brightly colored? The reason is that male birds often use their striking colors to attract females. Often they are the ones to begin the process of attracting a mate by picking out a good nest site. Then they fly around displaying their colors and singing. In many species, females seem to prefer the males with the brightest feathers and the prettiest song. Although the colorful bird risks getting eaten, the drab bird risks losing out on getting a mate.

In order to remain safe for at least part of the year, some male birds, like goldfinches, only wear their stunning feathers at breeding time. During the rest of the year, their colorful garb is replaced with plain, duller feathers, similar to those that adorn the females. For example, brilliant yellow goldfinches turn a drab brown during the winter months.

You may wonder why female birds don't need to look beautiful during the mating season. The reason is that female birds are usually the ones that do the choosing. A male bird will sing, flap his wings, and, if he is colorful, display his bright feathers in hopes of attracting a mate. A female bird will watch the males and choose the one whose display she likes best.

There is another reason why female birds rarely wear fancy coats. They need to be difficult to see because they are usually the ones who sit on their nests warming the eggs till they hatch. They are also the ones who usually stay with the hatchlings and feed them. If mother birds were brightly colored, they would quickly attract predators right to their nests and their helpless young. The female birds, therefore, must stay drab in order to keep both themselves and their eggs or hatchlings well hidden.

If you've spent time watching birds, you've probably noticed that in some species, such as song sparrows and pigeons, the male birds never become brightly colored. These males look exactly like females of their species, and the two sexes can only be told apart by song and behavior. It probably won't surprise you that in many of these species, the males share the job of parenting with the females. As a result, they need to remain drab in order to help hide their young. How, then, do ordinary looking males get the attention of a female? The answer is that they rely on beautiful songs and a variety of movements to attract their mates.

WHY DO BABY DUCKS FOLLOW THEIR MOTHER?

Even before they hatch from their eggs, baby ducks are learning who their mother is. A very powerful instinct tells ducklings and many other kinds of young fowl to notice and learn the features of the first creature they hear or see. Baby ducks may actually start to recognize their mother's clucking sounds before they hatch. They also learn to recognize their mother's face by the time they are a few hours old. Once the young have memorized their mother's features, instinct also tells them to always stay with her because they need her to survive.

Scientists call this special early learning by ducklings, goslings, and some other baby birds *imprinting*. Basically, it means that the particular characteristics of the parent become fixed, or imprinted, in an offspring's brain. (In the case of Canada geese and other species in which both parents raise their young, both are imprinted in their babies' brains.) Not only do the hatchlings note the appearance of the parent, but they also memorize the sound of its voice. Voice sounds are especially important for members of the wood duck species because their nests are tucked away in dark holes in trees and the ducklings can't see their parent very well.

The ability to imprint is vital for all bird species in which the young are *precocial*, or able to walk about and leave the nest shortly after hatching. Precocial species include not only ducklings and goslings, but baby chicks, turkeys, and pheasants. On the other hand, imprinting is not as important in robins, jays, and other *altricial* species, whose offspring emerge naked and helpless and remain in the nest awhile.

Imprinting is necessary for precocial hatchlings for several reasons. First, it insures that when the mother decides to leave the nest, her brood will automatically go along. Normally, ducks and geese abandon the nest when their offspring are only two or three days old. Imprinting also insures that if the young accidentally become mixed in with other adults of their species they will still be able to find "Mom."

Ducklings actually imprint best a few hours after they hatch. Within twenty-four hours of emerging, the young birds usually know their mother well enough to pick her out of a group. After these first hours have passed, their ability to imprint fades and they gradually lose it completely.

Scientists believe that the amazing abilities of newly hatched young to learn to recognize their parent is inborn. This means that young, precocial fowl imprint automatically without ever "thinking" about what they are doing. In fact, if their real parent isn't there, the first moving thing the hatchlings see may become fixed in their brains. Baby ducks hatched in an incubator have been known to fix on and follow the person who cares for them. Even more surprising, scientists have even been able to imprint motherless hatchlings on a red light bulb that makes quacking sounds.

HOW MANY EGGS CAN A CHICKEN LAY?

A single chicken could keep you in scrambled eggs all year long. Chickens can lay 5 to 7 eggs a week. An extra-good layer will produce more than 360 eggs in a year. However, a hen only keeps laying under one condition—her eggs must be removed from her after they are laid. If the hen feels eggs underneath her, she will stop making new ones and simply sit on the eggs until they hatch.

In order to make eggs, the chicken, like other vertebrates, or animals with backbones, depends on two special organs, an *ovary* and an *oviduct*. The ovary is a special organ where female animals make eggs. Hens have a single ovary that is filled with lots of eggs at all different stages of growth.

The immature eggs are clumped together so that they look like a bunch of grapes. Each day, one egg reaches its full size. This mature egg lacks a shell and is mostly a ball of yolk. It bursts out of the ovary and moves into a long, open tube called the oviduct.

In many female animals the oviduct is just a simple tube that carries eggs. But in birds the oviduct is also a marvelous shell-making machine. Each part of the tube has its own special function. At the top of the tube is a large cup called the *infundibulum*. If the hen has mated with a rooster, the male's sperm will meet the shell-less egg in the infundibulum. If the egg has been fertilized by sperm it can get covered with shell and may eventually develop into a chick. It probably seems confusing, but the fertilized, yolky egg together with the shell that surrounds it is also called an egg. If the hen's yolky egg does not get fertilized, however, it will still get covered with shell before it leaves the chicken. The eggs that we buy in the supermarket have unfertilized, yolky "eggs" inside them.

The yolky egg, fertilized or unfertilized, moves from the infundibulum to the *magnum*. In this section, the yolky ball is covered with egg white, or *albumen*. After four hours of collecting egg white, the yolk and white pass on to the *isthmus*, a word that means passage. Here two thin membranes are formed to cover the egg. The two membranes create a double layer of protection for the chick. They are designed to be tough enough to keep the growing embryo from losing water, while also being

Ovary and Oviduct of Chicken

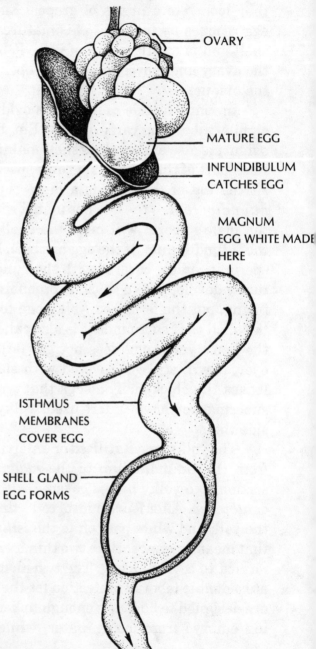

OVARY

MATURE EGG

INFUNDIBULUM
CATCHES EGG

MAGNUM
EGG WHITE MADE
HERE

ISTHMUS
MEMBRANES
COVER EGG

SHELL GLAND
EGG FORMS

thin enough to allow oxygen and carbon dioxide to pass through so that the embryo can breathe.

The final stage in egg formation lasts about twenty hours. It takes place in a round segment of the oviduct called the *shell gland*. In this region, water and salt are pumped in through the membranes. This salty fluid thins the egg white, providing a liquid that surrounds and cushions the embryo. Lastly, a shell forms to cover the egg. Completely enclosed in its protective coat, the egg is then finally ready to be laid.

WHY DON'T WOODPECKERS GET HEADACHES FROM PECKING TREES?

Even thinking about using our heads as hammers may give us humans a headache. But woodpeckers bang their bills against wood several hundred times a day and aren't bothered a bit.

What's more, these birds hammer incredibly fast and hard. Each peck takes only one thousandth of a second, and the woodpecker's beak moves up and down at a rate of more than twenty feet per second! Scientists have estimated that the impact of this high-speed hammering results in a force against the bird's head that is more than a hundred times greater than the pressure astronauts experience as they lift off into space!

How do woodpeckers keep from getting punchy from the poundings? Part of the answer lies in the way their heads are designed. Woodpeckers' brains are very lightweight and fit snugly in a casing of extra-tough, spongy bone. The tight packing keeps the brain from being jiggled about, and the bony covering helps absorb the force of the blows.

The precise way woodpeckers go about pounding also helps prevent injury. After lining up the target and perhaps taking a light practice stroke or two, a bird holds its head rigid and hammers absolutely straight up and down. Thus, the woodpecker's head doesn't jerk from side to side and jolt its brain. The pecking bird also avoids jolts by using its stiff tail feathers to brace itself firmly against the tree.

WHY DON'T PENGUINS FREEZE IN THE COLD?

In the middle of the Antarctic winter, when the sun shines only a few hours daily and temperatures drop to fifty degrees below zero, Emperor penguins are alive and well and maintaining a body temperature of over one hundred degrees. The reason these hardy birds not only survive but stay so warm in the bitter weather is that they are specially designed for the climate.

For one thing, these cold-loving creatures have a lot of insulation in the form of fat. A thick layer of fat lying just beneath the surface of a penguin's skin helps block out the cold and hold in body heat. This protective fat, or blubber, is the reason penguins appear plumper and rounder than most birds.

Penguins also come equipped with an extra-thick covering of insulating feathers on their bodies. Right next to the skin are soft, fluffy tufts that trap air warmed by the birds' own body heat. This down is a little like penguin long underwear. On top of the tufts are very small, densely packed, oily feathers. These grow so close together that there may be up to seventy of them in a square inch. The smooth, slick coat formed by these feathers looks almost like a hide and provides a perfect barrier against water and wind, as well as cold. As further protection against the harsh environment, some kinds of penguins even have feathers over their noses. This helps warm the air before they breathe it and prevents snow from blowing into their nostrils.

Penguins' feet are not well insulated like their bodies, but nevertheless, these parts are designed for the cold. As a penguin stands or swims in icy water, the temperature of its feet may drop to thirty-two degrees—nearly freezing. In such conditions a human's feet would become frostbitten. The tissues of a penguin's feet, however, can tolerate such temperatures without being injured. A special set of blood vessels carries just enough heat to the bird's feet to prevent them from freezing.

Another design feature that helps penguins survive the extreme temperatures is their black and white coloring. If you have ever studied the characteristics of colors in science class, you may know that different hues have differing capacities to absorb and deflect, or turn back, the heat energy of sunlight. Black absorbs the most heat energy; white absorbs the least. Thus, when a penguin wants to catch some rays to warm itself, it hunches down and turns its light-absorbing black back toward the sun. If, on the other hand, the bird wants to cool off a little, it turns its light-deflecting white chest toward the sun.

HOW CAN PARROTS TALK?

Parrots and a few other "talking" birds are able to do something no other creatures can. They can imitate human words and phrases so well that it seems as though a person is speaking.

Part of the reason these feathered friends can do this is that birds have very good hearing and sound-learning abilities. Even birds that don't usually mimic humans pay careful attention to the songs sung by other members of their species. They quickly begin to repeat these sound patterns themselves. This ability is very important, since many birds depend on their song to advertise for a mate and defend their territory (see "Do Birds Sing Because They're Happy?" on page 65).

Physically, birds tend to be good mimics because they have very sophisticated sound-making equipment. In fact, birds' sound-producing apparatus, the *syrinx*, is every bit as flexible and useful to them as the human equipment, the *larynx*, is to us.

For example, our larynx is a muscular, boxlike chamber with an opening at the bottom and top. Stretched across the top opening of this voice box are some tough, stringy strips of tissue called *vocal cords*. Sounds are made when puffs of air pass up through the chamber and cause the vocal cords to vibrate. Muscles tighten or loosen the vocal cords to produce a range of low to high sounds.

The bird's syrinx contains two complete sets of sound-making parts, one associated with each *bronchial tube*, the long tubes that carry air to the lungs. Each of the bird's sound-making sets has its own sound generator, or membrane, as well as a nervous system and controlling muscles. This means a bird can make two entirely different sounds at the same time—something we humans can't do.

The bird's process of sound production is complicated, and scientists are still investigating how it works. Basically, it appears that the sound-making membrane is pushed out into the bronchial tube. This stops the air from flowing by. Then special muscles pull the membrane back again, allowing the blocked air to rush past. This causes the membrane to move back and forth, or vibrate, which produces sound. You can imagine that this complex method gives birds a lot of control and flexibility in producing sounds, and a number of birds, such as mockers and bowerbirds, put their talent to work mimicking whistles, horn honks, dog barks, and the songs of other bird species.

On the other hand, only the parrot and a few other species can imitate human speech. One reason is that sound waves produced by the human voice are normally pitched lower, or vibrate less rapidly, than the sounds produced by most birds. In addition, the sounds produced by the human voice box are not simply released like a bird's notes,

Bird's Voice Box

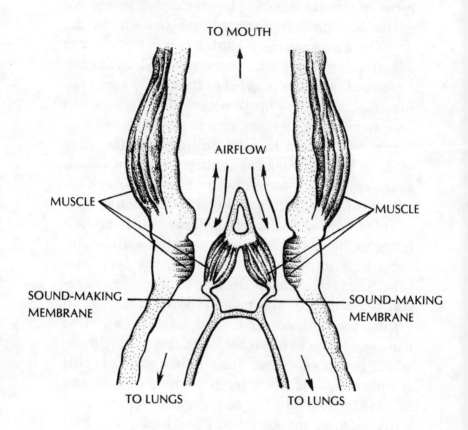

TO MOUTH

AIRFLOW

MUSCLE

MUSCLE

SOUND-MAKING
MEMBRANE

SOUND-MAKING
MEMBRANE

TO LUNGS

TO LUNGS

SYRINX

but are shaped by the mouth and tongue into speech. Parrots have the ability to produce the lower-pitched sounds required to mimic human speech because their bodies are large and their natural "voices" are low compared to most other birds. Parrots are also able to shape these sounds to suggest speech better than most birds because they have unusually large mouths and tongues.

Now that you know how parrots are able to imitate human speech, you might be wondering *why* they do it. Surprisingly, scientists say that parrots never use their incredible ability to imitate other species except when they are living with humans. In the wild, parrots live with their mates in large, noisy, sociable flocks. They use their wonderful listening and sound-making skills only to recognize and imitate their mate's call and to communicate with others of their own kind. Researchers now believe that these birds may imitate human speech as a substitute for the "bird talk" they would normally enjoy in the wild. Mimicking human words and phrases may serve as a way for parrots to form close relationships, or bonds, with their keepers.

HOW DO RATTLESNAKES RATTLE?

When a rattlesnake rattles its rattle, it's really just snapping its skin. The rattlesnake's noisy tailpiece is actually a chain of rings, or *segments*, made of hardened skin. They are loosely held together so that when they are shaken, the segments bump against each other and make a sound.

A baby rattlesnake does not come into the world with a working rattle. A rattle segment forms a little later, when the young snake first sheds its skin. After this, each time the snake sheds its skin again, a new segment is added. Each new segment is a little bit bigger than the one made before it. Thus, the rattle ends up with big rings near the body and smaller and smaller rings near the tip.

A rattlesnake sheds its skin and makes new rattle segments several times a year; it will make about thirty new rattle segments during its lifetime. The snake, however, doesn't usually keep every part it makes. As the rattle becomes long, its segments tend to get scraped on rocks and worn off. Thus, the rattle of a wild snake is rarely more than eight segments long.

If you've never heard a rattlesnake's rattle you might guess that it would sound like a baby's rattling toy. Actually, the rattlesnake shakes its tail so quickly that all its snaps blend together. What you hear is a loud buzz or hiss. The buzz is startling enough to frighten off most of the rattlesnakes' enemies. The rattle seems to serve as the rattlesnake's own built-in warning device.

WHY DOES A SNAKE FLICK ITS TONGUE?

A snake uses its tongue to "smell" the air. When it sticks out its forked tongue in a flicking motion it is actually picking up the smelly chemical particles that are given off by all animals, plants, and objects. It is these particles that give things their special scents. Humans smell an object when the particles it gives off enter their noses and turn on special smelling cells. Snakes smell objects this way, too, but they also have an extra set of smelling cells located in the roofs of their mouths. By using their tongues, snakes can pick up and carry odor particles to the extra smelling cells. This second smelling organ gives snakes superior smelling abilities.

Whenever a snake needs more information about the area around it, it darts its tongue through a notch in the upper jaw. The tip of the tongue is moist, so odor particles readily cling to it. A quick jerk brings the tongue back inside and places the particles into the special chemical sensing organ on the roof of the mouth. This special packet of smelling cells is called *Jacobson's organ.*

Snakes are not the only creatures with a Jacobson's organ. Although we humans don't have it, this special smell detector is found in most amphibians, reptiles, and mammals. It is believed that Jacobson's organ helps animals to smell their food once it enters the mouth. However, snakes and their close relatives, the lizards, with their flicking tongues, can also use Jacobson's organ to pick up smells outside of their mouths. Thus, these reptiles are particularly good at smelling the world around them.

HOW DO SNAKES SWALLOW THINGS BIGGER THAN THEIR HEADS?

Snakes are animals with very small heads but very big mouths. The amazing ability of some snakes to swallow eggs, birds, squirrels, and even small pigs, results from the special design of the snake's jaw. The best way to understand how this jaw works is to compare it with our own.

In humans, the jaw is pretty simple. It is made up of two bones that connect tightly to the skull and one fairly moveable lower bone that lets us chew and talk. In contrast, the snake jaw is complex, containing as many as sixteen bones. In many species, such as vipers, cobras, and rattlesnakes, these jaw bones are specially designed for swallowing large prey. The bones that form the upper jaw are not tightly fitted to the rest of the skull bones, as they are in humans. Instead, they are loose enough that they can move separately from the rest of the skull. In addition, in snakes both the upper and lower jaws consist of two separate halves, and the bones of the lower jaw are held together by a very stretchy ligament.

When a loose-jawed snake opens its mouth to swallow prey, it thrusts its upper jaw bones up and out while it pulls its lower jaw down. This creates a very large opening, allowing the animal to stretch its mouth over its prize.

Next, the snake "walks" the halves of its jaws along the food. Each half of each jaw moves forward separately, pulling the prey in the direction of the throat. The snake's sharp teeth, which point backwards, help to pull the prey along.

Once a snake has "walked" its prey back toward its throat, it must then swallow the food. Several special design features make swallowing bulky prey easy. First of all, the snake has a very

Snake Swallowing an Egg

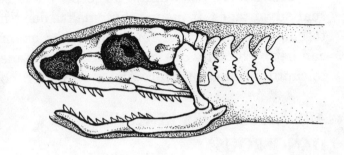

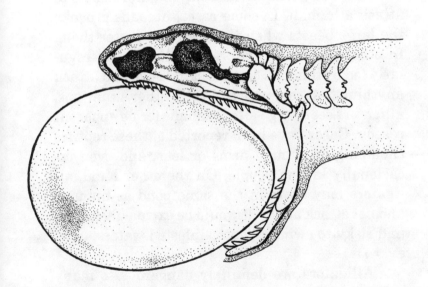

elastic skin, which can stretch around the prey as it moves down the throat. Secondly, the snake has the remarkable ability to move its *trachea*, or windpipe, out of its mouth into the air, so that the opening is not blocked by food. This enables the animal to continue to breathe while it eats.

The ability to swallow large prey has some real advantages. It means that snakes don't need to eat very often. The rattlesnake, for example, can get by on only one meal a year if it manages to capture something nice and big like a rabbit!

ARE ALLIGATORS REALLY DANGEROUS?

Humans aren't at the top of the alligator hit list, but they do occasionally become targets. Nobody knows exactly what makes an alligator decide to attack a human. In some cases, humans provoke the large beasts when they tease or pester them. In other instances, 'gators that have been regularly fed by humans become aggressive and attack anything that comes near. In still other situations, alligators seem to go after humans for no apparent reason. Cases have been reported of these reptiles chomping on human arms or legs, and even occasionally killing people. On the other hand, alligators may swim in the same pond as humans and not attack at all. (It would be extremely foolish and risky to swim in 'gator-infested waters, however.)

Alligators are definitely dangerous to many animals, though, since they normally feed on such species as fish, birds, frogs, raccoons, dogs, and deer. Sometimes they also become cannibalistic, capturing and eating smaller alligators.

The alligator's skill in catching and eating

large prey results, in part, from the size of its body. A fully mature adult male may be ten feet from snout to tail and weigh over five hundred pounds.

The 'gator also has very powerful jaws that aid it in catching a meal. It has an extra-strong mouth grip, and its sharp teeth can crunch down on a victim with nearly one thousand pounds of force. As soon as the alligator has gotten a good grip, it tries to drown its victim in the water. This task is made easier by the fact that the alligator's nose is placed on top of its head. This means that it can drag its prey under the water while still keeping its nostrils above the surface.

Once its victim is dead, the alligator will break its dinner up into eatable parts. Because the 'gator lacks the flat grinding teeth that mammals have for chewing, it does not bite off and chew small pieces of meat. Instead, the powerful predator twists its own body around and around or twists the prey with its mouth and breaks off chunks, which it then swallows whole.

HOW DO CHAMELEONS CHANGE COLOR?

A chameleon doesn't need to be a magician to change its colors. It's got all the equipment it needs packed right into its skin. This type of lizard carries packets of color in special skin cells called *chromatophores*. Now there's nothing remarkable about that, because most animals have color-carrying cells. What is remarkable is that chameleons have chromatophores that can actually change colors.

These special color-carrying cells are also found in a number of other lizards, amphibians, and fish, which can also change their skin colors. The chameleon, however, is one of the most skillful quick-change artists.

A chameleon's chromatophores come in a number of different colors, including red, brown, yellow, and white. The different colored cells are stacked in layers in the chameleon's skin. Their colors all combine to give it its special shade.

One layer of the chameleon's skin contains special chromatophores called *melanophores*. It is these star-shaped cells that hold the secret to color change. The melanophores are filled with tiny granules of a chemical called *melanin*. Melanin can create colors like brown, black, or gray. The melanophores are able to cause color changes because they contain melanin granules that can move.

Here's how the color changes work. When the melanophore's granules are packed into the center of the cell, the long arms of the star-shaped melanophores become clear. This allows the blues or yellows of cells beneath the melanophores to show through. When the melanin granules are spread throughout the cell, however, they hide the colors of the other cells. Then the darker colors in the melanophores make the animal's skin look brown or red. The movement of the granules is controlled by the chameleon's nervous system.

There are lots of different things that can cause an animal to change its color. Chameleons, which are found mainly in Africa and Madagascar, seem to change their colors in response to temperature, light, and their emotional state. They generally wear a coat of brown with red stripes when they are at rest in the morning. As the day advances, the changeable animals will take on a grayish-green or olive-brown color. If frightened, chameleons rapidly turn a pale green with white stripes. These color changes may help to hide the animal among the trees and leaves in its native habitat. They also seem to work to communicate messages like "I am ready to fight" to other chameleons.

HOW DOES A FROG CATCH FLIES WITH ITS TONGUE?

A frog has its own special bug zapper right in its mouth. In less than a tenth of a second, its tongue can shoot out, snap an unsuspecting fly or other insect, and snap back into its mouth again.

The tongues of many frogs and toads are cleverly designed for catching prey. For one thing, they're coated with a sticky mucus. This makes them work like fly paper. Whenever an insect touches the sticky surface, it gets stuck, at least for an instant. This gives the frog time to pull its tongue back into its mouth before the victim can escape.

The way some frogs' and toads' tongues fit into their mouths also aids in catching a meal. In contrast to human tongues, which are attached at the back of the mouth, the tongues of these creatures are often attached at the front. This makes it quick and easy to flip the tongue forward and out into the air.

As a further aid to hunting, the tongues of many species are exceptionally long and flexible. For example, the American toad can stretch out its personal bug catcher more than two inches. Such a long reach helps these amphibians snare victims that seem too far away to be caught. Some frogs and toads are even able to curl a rubbery tongue around a victim and draw it into the mouth.

Of course, speed and accuracy are also essential to making a catch. Frogs and toads come equipped with a set of strong muscles to propel the tongue out rapidly in exactly the right direction and then snap it back before dinner escapes. Sci-

Toad and Frog Catching a Meal

entists who have observed these insect eaters hunting say they almost never miss a shot.

CAN TOADS GIVE YOU WARTS?

Toads are warty, but they can't give you warts. Although toad warts and human warts may seem similar, they are not at all alike. The warts on human skin are caused by a virus that can spread from one place to another. On the other hand, the small raised areas on many species of toads and a few frogs are simply a normal part of the skin. Toad warts are actually tiny chemical-producing sacs, or glands. Normally, there are a number of very small glands sprinkled over the toad's body, as well as a pair of slightly bigger glands that are located on each side of its head.

While they may look unattractive to us, these warty glands can be a real lifesaver for a toad or frog. That's because they often produce chemicals that help protect these soft-bodied amphibians from their enemies. For example, in a number of species the glands release a substance that has a foul odor or irritates the skin of an attacker. In other species, such as the Arizona toad and the marine toad, the glands secrete a powerful, nasty-tasting poison during an attack. This usually makes the enemy spit out its potential victim. It can also cause vomiting or even death in a predator as big as a dog. Additionally, a few species, such as the poisonous arrow frogs of Central and South America, produce such a deadly poison that less than a tiny drop can kill an average-sized human. Predators who make the mistake of attacking these little amphibians do not live to try it again.

WHY DO FISH SWIM IN SCHOOLS?

Swimming along in a soldierlike unit, or *schooling*, just comes naturally to many fish. In fact, about twenty thousand different species spend at least part of their time swimming in the orderly formation of a school. Normally, schooling involves fish of the same size and species, evenly spaced and all going in the same direction at the same speed. Schools may have only a few members or millions of them. Sometimes a school is so big that it stretches for several miles.

Since schooling is so common among fish, scientists think it must offer protection or other advantages, but nobody is absolutely certain. One suggestion for why fish school is that a school may look like a single gigantic creature to predators and, therefore, they may be afraid to attack. Another idea is that the school serves as a warning system for its members. While each individual fish can only keep watch for predators in the area right around it, all the "schoolmates" together can guard a very large space. Moreover, the reaction of one fish to danger quickly warns all the rest of the school to flee.

Still another possible advantage of the school is that predators become confused by so many targets and can't decide which victim to chase. This "confusion effect" has actually been tested by putting a single fish in a tank with a predator fish, and then putting an entire school in with a predator. When faced with a single target, a predator usually snapped it up in about thirty seconds. However, making a catch was generally more difficult when a predator was confronted with a school of fish. A typical predator wasted nearly two and a half minutes chasing several different individuals before finally making a catch. While two and a half minutes may not seem like much time to you, it gives the entire school a good opportunity to scatter and escape.

Life in a group also seems to have other benefits for fish besides protection. Researchers have found that fish in schools can swim longer, stand more cold, and cover more territory than individuals traveling alone. Groups also seem to require less oxygen per fish than individual members left alone.

In case you're wondering exactly *how* fish manage to glide, dive, and even turn together so precisely, scientists have studied that, too. They have learned that there isn't a leader directing school movements. Nor is there a special group communication system telling all the members what to do. Instead, each fish gets clues from the others around it and then immediately adjusts its position and speed to theirs. The individual fish uses two main senses to keep itself in line. It depends on its eyes to determine the distance and angle to its neighbors. And it uses a special motion-sensing system called the *lateral line* to pick up the movements of the other fish.

The lateral line system is a series of tiny holes

that runs down the length of both sides of the fish. Inside the holes are special nerve cells that sense the movements of water around the fish. As neighboring fish change their speed or direction, they cause the water to move. This motion is detected by the lateral line system. It lets a fish actually feel the movements of its neighbors so it can position its own body in line with theirs.

CAN YOU GET A SHOCK FROM AN ELECTRIC FISH?

An electric eel is a truly shocking fish. With the ability to produce more than five hundred volts of electricity, this freshwater fish could give you a powerful shock. Normally, however, the electric eel uses its zapping power to kill the small fish and amphibians that it uses for food. The eel's strong electric pulse is also useful in keeping larger predators away.

The ability to produce electricity is not as strange as it seems. Actually, all animals produce electricity inside their bodies. It is this electricity that enables our nerves and muscles to work. However, the electric eel is special in its ability to generate electricity outside of its body.

The sluggish electric eel produces its powerful pulse in a pair of special organs that run most of the length of its long tail. These organs are made up of flat muscle cells that are arranged like a stack of plates. Each muscle plate produces a small pulse of electricity. Because the eel fires thousands

Electric Fish

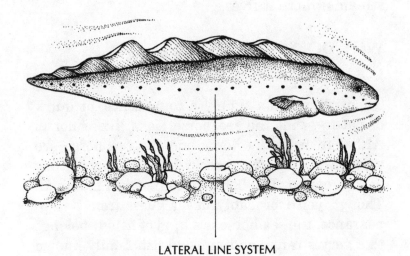

LATERAL LINE SYSTEM

of plates at the same time, many small pulses combine to produce one big charge.

The electric eel's remarkable weapon has a special added benefit. Its strong pulse extends several yards into the water, so a victim does not even need to touch the eel to get a jolt.

Electric eels are not the only creatures that generate electricity. The electric catfish and the electric ray, or torpedo, also produce a powerful charge. In addition, there are a number of small African fish that are weakly electric. These fish, which include the knife fish and the elephant longnose, produce much less than one volt of electricity. This is too weak to shock other animals. However, such weak pulses are useful for communication and as a special kind of locating device, enabling a fish to "see" electrically in the muddy streams where it lives.

WHY DOES A SEA HORSE LOOK LIKE A HORSE?

Scientists say it's simply a coincidence, or quirk of nature, that the sea horse looks like a horse. Although both the horse and the sea horse are vertebrates, or creatures with backbones, they aren't related. The horse, of course, is a mammal. Though you'd probably never guess from its appearance, the sea horse is a kind of fish. It belongs to a very strange and unusual fish family known as *Syngnathidae*.

One prominent feature that makes the sea horse and its close relatives appear "horsey" instead of "fishy" is a long, noselike part on the front of the head. This snout may look like a horse's muzzle, but it definitely isn't one. The horse's muzzle includes mouth parts that it uses for chewing food and nostrils for breathing air. The sea horse, on the other hand, doesn't have a nose for inhaling air because it obtains oxygen from water by using its gills. The snout doesn't have mouth parts like a horse's muzzle either. The opening is toothless and the jaws are fused together and don't move. In fact, the long structure is actually a food tube the sea horse uses to suck up its meals. It draws in tiny shrimp, insects, and plants and sends them directly to its *gullet*, or stomach. It also draws in water and forces it through gills to extract the oxygen needed for life.

Another characteristic that gives the sea horse a horsey rather than fishy appearance is its graceful, curving "neck" and "mane." Actually, the neck is not smooth and fleshy like a horse's. It is covered with a hard outer skeleton that is made up of a series of bony plates. The sea horse's mane is a set of knobby spines.

Even if it didn't have some horsey looking features, the sea horse would still be a very weird fish. Instead of the usual finned tail, it has a long,

Sea Horse

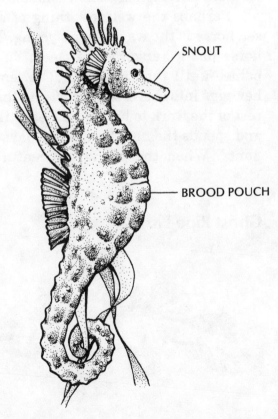

SNOUT

BROOD POUCH

thin, flexible one. It uses this handy appendage to hold onto things such as seaweed or coral, and to float upright.

Unlike most fish, the sea horse is a poor swimmer, and it isn't very good at chasing down prey. As a result, it obtains its food simply by sucking in edibles that happen to drift by. Since it also swims too poorly to succeed in escaping from most enemies, it tries to blend into the environment and avoid being seen. Some species of sea horses blend in by changing their colors like chameleons. (See "How Do Chameleons Change Color?" on page 85 for more information on how animals change color.)

Perhaps the weirdest thing of all about the sea horse is the way it bears young. The male sea horse has a kangaroolike pouch for carrying its babies until they are born. The female deposits her eggs into this *brood pouch* and then leaves the rest of the work to her mate. He fertilizes the eggs and spends the next ten to fifty days being "pregnant." When the young are mature enough to

Ghost Pipe Fish

survive on their own, the male tightens the muscles of his pouch and pushes the young *fry*, or baby fish, out into their watery world.

Although it's quite difficult to look at a sea horse and imagine how it fits into the fish family, studying its long-ago ancestor, the ghost pipefish, gives some clues. You can clearly see that this now-extinct creature is a fish, but it also has a sea horse-like head and extra-long, thin tail. Its appearance suggests that over time, the strange little sea horse *evolved*, or developed, from a creature like this.

INDEX